Michel Foucault

David Macey

LEARNING RESOURCES
CENTRE

Havering College
of Further and Higher education

HAVERING
COLLEGE

REAKTION BOOKS

194

H·L

161695

For you, Margaret

Published by Reaktion Books Ltd
79 Farringdon Road
London EC1M 3JU, UK

www.reaktionbooks.co.uk

First published 2004

Copyright © David Macey 2004

All rights reserved
No part of this publication may be reproduced, stored in a retrieval system,
or transmitted, in any form or by any means, electronic, mechanical,
photocopying, recording or otherwise, without the prior permission
of the publishers.

Printed and bound by Biddles Ltd, Kings's Lynn

British Library Cataloguing in Publication Data
Macey, David, 1949–
    Michel Foucault. – (Critical lives)
    1. Foucault, Michel 2. Philosophers – France – Biography
    I. Title
    194

ISBN 1 86189 226 8

Michel Foucault

Titles in the series Critical Lives present the work of leading cultural figures of the modern period. Each book explores the life of the artist, writer, philosopher or architect in question and relates it to their major works.

In the same series

Jean Genet
Stephen Barber

Pablo Picasso
Mary Ann Caws

Contents

One 7

Two 27

Three 46

Four 63

Five 84

Six 105

Seven 126

References 147
Select Bibliography 156
Photo Acknowledgements 160

One

There is a rue du Dr Foucault in the centre of Nanterre. The street was named in honour of Paul Foucault, a nineteenth-century physician who devoted his life to caring for the poor of what was still an agricultural village and not yet a suburb of Paris. Almost nothing is known about him except that he died penniless, as befits a doctor who treated his patients at little or no cost. The only thing he bequeathed to his family was a silver pen presented to him by a delegation of grateful patients. It remained in the family for three generations but was eventually stolen during a burglary and has never been recovered. The victim of the burglary was Denys Foucault, the younger brother of Paul-Michel Foucault.[1]

Michel Foucault and his siblings were not children of Paris and its suburbs. They were born into a wealthy provincial family living in Poitiers, some 300 kilometres to the south-west of the capital. Born in 1900, Foucault's mother, Anne Malapert, was the daughter of a surgeon and anatomist who taught at the city's medical school. Her family was rich and well connected. Her cousin Jean Plattard had taught at the local university before being appointed to a post at the Sorbonne in Paris, where he won a solid reputation for his scholarly editions of Rabelais, Montaigne and other Renaissance authors. Her brother Paulin taught philosophy at a Paris *lycée*. He held a doctorate and was the author of a well-respected philosophy textbook published in 1907. Her brother Roger opted for a military career, rose to the rank of colonel, and fought with great distinction

A general view of Poitiers, the setting for a provincial childhood.

during the First World War. Her family owned land and a large house known as Le Piroir in the village of Vendeuvre-du-Poitiers, 18 kilometres outside Poitiers. The house still stands in its own grounds at the end of a long drive lined with lime trees. Impressive rather than conventionally beautiful, it is built from the local limestone, which is porous, and therefore had problems with damp. By the time that Anne was born, her family had accumulated sufficient wealth to build a large white house at 10 rue Arthur Ranc in the centre of Poitiers. It was here that Paul-Michel Foucault was born on 15 October 1926. He was the second of three children.

In 1924 Anne Malapert married Paul-André Foucault, who was seven years older than she. Born in Fontainebleau, he was, like his father and grandfather before him, a doctor. He had served in the army during the Great War and had been awarded the Croix de guerre. After moving to Poitiers, he worked at the Hôtel-Dieu hospital, where he acquired a good reputation as an anatomist, and had a private surgical practice. The Foucault and Malapert practices eventually merged and prospered. The new practice extended far beyond Poitiers itself and covered a wide rural area.

Dr Foucault and his wife had contacts, both professional and personal, with the Benedictine community at St Martin's Abbey in nearby Ligugé. The size of the practice meant that Dr Foucault worked long hours and was often away from home; the state of medical technology was such that a folding operating table had to be carried in the boot of one of the two cars he ran. When necessary, his driver doubled as an anaesthetist.

The Foucault family was by no means aristocratic, but both Foucault's father and mother were local *notables* and respected citizens. Their wealth derived from the classic combination of fees from a liberal profession and land-owning. All that was needed to complete the picture of provincial prosperity was a lawyer in the family. By the 1930s they could afford to purchase a holiday home in La Baule on the Atlantic coast. The town, with its broad sweep of sand and its pines, is now a rather exclusive and expensive resort; in the 1930s it was relatively undeveloped, although it already had a casino, and was frequented mainly by middle-class families from Nantes and Saint-Nazaire.

Foucault's mother would have liked to become a doctor, but convention was against her: women of her class and background did not work. Her considerable energies were therefore invested in her family. She ran the household and its servants single-handed and, with the help of a secretary, effectively managed the practice. This was important: a doctor was a businessman as well as a physician. She also took sole responsibility for the care of her children. Both she and her husband were very ambitious for their children, and quite prepared to exploit their numerous family and professional connections on their behalf.

Paul-Michel Foucault was the child of a family that enjoyed both social prestige and social power. The house in the rue Arthur Ranc was spacious enough for each of the three children to have their own bedroom. There was a garden, and cats and dogs were in

St Porchaire, Poitiers: Mass on Sundays.

permanent residence. The family was respectable, politically con-
servative and church-going in a fairly conventional fashion, though
it was usually their grandmother who took the children to Sunday
mass at Saint-Porchaire in the city centre. Paul-Michel was also the
child of a family with a strong sense of tradition. Eldest sons were
always called 'Paul', usually with a second hyphenated forename –
the 'Michel' was his mother's idea. And they became doctors and
surgeons.

   The capital of the Vienne *département*, Poitiers, stands on a
rocky promontory at the confluence of the rivers Clain and Boivre.

In the mid-1920s it had a population of just over 40,000, virtually no industry and was dependent for its wealth on its rich agricultural hinterland. Many found the town to be introverted and indifferent or even hostile to outsiders. Some had the impression that nothing had happened there for hundreds of years. The city's rich heritage and particularly the façades of its many Romanesque churches bore witness to a glorious past, but it was now little more than a sleepy provincial backwater. Its medieval streets and alleys were not yet the tourist attraction they have become. The medical school taught only the first three years of the traditional degree, and students then had to transfer elsewhere to complete their course.

Despite the air of somnolence, things did happen in Poitiers. The rue Arthur Ranc was formerly known as the rue de la Visitation. As they walked past the building at number 21, Paul-Michel and Denys, who was his junior by seven years, would whisper, 'That's where it happened.' On 23 May 1901 the police, acting on the basis of an anonymous tip-off, broke into the house. In a second-floor room with barred windows they found an emaciated woman with hair down to her thighs lying in her own excrement. She was the 50-year-old Blanche Monnier. Rumours immediately began to spread, and they were all the more scandalous in that the family was so respectable: Monnier's father was once dean of the University's Faculty of Arts. Blanche had supposedly had a clandestine affair with a local lawyer and had given birth to an illegitimate child. When her brother and mother went on trial for her false imprisonment, the crowds outside the Palais de Justice bayed for blood. Postcards showing the house circulated widely, while papers like *L'Illustration* and *La Vie illustrée* published lurid engravings and photographs of the discovery of Monnier. Broadsheets with the words to maudlin laments were sold in the streets. In 1930 the novelist André Gide published the definitive documentary account of the case, simply entitled *La Séquestrée de Poitiers*. Mme Monnier died before she could come to trial but Blanche Monnier's brother

The lycée, Poitiers. The Foucault children are born to learn.

was acquitted on appeal. There had been no false imprisonment. Monnier had been anorexic and had experienced a strange form of mysticism resulting in serious depression and a withdrawal from the world. Hospitalization did improve her physical condition, but she never recovered her reason and died in 1913. That the Foucault family did not know the story is inconceivable; that they did not talk about it is perfectly conceivable.

Foucault very rarely spoke of his childhood, but in 1975 he told a radio interviewer that he sometimes had the impression that he had grown up in an environment in which the rule of existence lay in knowledge. It was a competitive environment in which the one thing that counted was knowing more than anyone else, performing better that anyone else.[2] His brother confirms this: the Foucault children were 'born to learn' and they were expected to succeed. This is no exaggeration. Foucault started school at the age of four. When Francine entered the elementary class of the Lycée Henri-IV, he simply refused to be separated from his adored sister, who was two years older than he. Thanks to a special dispensation, he was allowed to sit at the back of the class. The lonely-looking boy was left largely to his own devices, but he did learn to read. Throughout his childhood and adolescence, school was his life. He had few outside interests. Paul-Michel did enjoy tennis, but his poor eyesight and glasses left him at a disadvantage on the court. He also enjoyed cycling, and often rode out to see his grandmother at Le Piroir. The centre of Poitiers was densely populated, and space was at a premium. Le Piroir offered the room to play and to run. There was also the further and very special attraction of riding Cyrano the donkey.

The children's education continued at home: private piano lessons were a matter of course. In 1936 an English nanny joined the household to give the children conversation lessons. Foucault does not seem to have benefited greatly from her presence, and it was only when he began to visit the United States regularly in the 1970s that he perfected his English. There was little entertainment apart from cards, books and the radio in the evening. A trip to the cinema to see *Snow White and the Seven Dwarfs* (1937) was a rare event, and one to be remembered for a long time. Dr Foucault's social position meant that he was under an obligation to entertain, although Denys Foucault recalls that the guests were always the same, as was the conversation. The children did not enjoy receiving guests. At times, they had to remain silent; at others, they had to make polite conversation with adults they scarcely knew. Very formal occasions were preferable, as they meant that the children ate separately and in a much more relaxed atmosphere.[3] Talk about personal matters was discouraged, and conversation focused on the children's school results. In a lecture delivered to the Collège de France in March 1982, Foucault reminded his audience – many of whom were far too young to know it from personal experience – that in his day the education of a child was primarily an apprenticeship in silence: the idea that a child could freely express himself at school was banished from the education system.[4]

Paul-Michel's progress through the school system was at first steady and encouraging. He entered the Lycée Henri-IV proper in 1936. He was an able and popular pupil and was regularly either at or very near the top of his class. The world seemed safe and predictable. Yet, even as a boy, Foucault did sense that the outside world was impinging on his life, and he found it threatening. In a surprisingly candid interview given in 1983, he spoke of remembering the assassination of Chancellor Dollfuss of Austria in 1934, and the arrival in Poitiers of refugees fleeing the Civil War in Spain. Increasingly, the threat of war felt like the framework of his existence. All young people were, he recalled, worried and the adult world had demonstrated to them that they had 'no refuge'.[5] He was well aware of the possibility of dying in an air raid. He was not sure whether he would grow up French or German.[6] In 1940 the threat of war materialized. As the German army advanced rapidly through Belgium and northern France, the roads were flooded with fleeing civilians who did not really know where they were going, and with demoralized and disorganized army units, many of them leaderless. On 17 June Marshall Pétain requested an armistice and told what remained of the army that the time had come to give up the fight. France was going to collaborate with Germany. Large areas of the north and the east were annexed by the Germans, and the rest of the country was divided into an occupied zone and a free zone with the spa town of Vichy as its capital. Poitiers was just inside the occupied zone and German soldiers patrolled its streets.

Members of the Paris branch of the family began to straggle into Poitiers in the early summer of 1940 and were accommodated at Le Piroir. The refugees included a newly qualified doctor named Jacqueline Verdeaux. Inter-family connections meant that she already knew the Foucaults, and as a very young girl she had sat on the knee of Colonel Malapert. Although she had only limited medical experience, she was immediately pressed into service by Dr Foucault, who had established a rudimentary field hospital in a requisitioned school. Her stay in Poitiers was short, because she soon headed south, but it was long enough to allow her to glimpse Paul-Michel at his sister's birthday party: a quizzical-looking boy already wearing glasses, and still in short trousers.

Although the family was quietly opposed to the Vichy government of collaboration, it conformed to the demands of the moment. There was no public expression of their pro-Allied views. There could not be any: German officers were billeted at Le Piroir until they were posted to the Eastern front. They had, recalls Denys Foucault, been given strict orders to be *Korrect*, and they obeyed them to the letter. Pictures of Pétain went up in the classrooms of Henri-iv and Paul-Michel's days now began with the ritual singing of a sickly hymn to the Marshall's glory: *Maréchal, nous voilà*.

Although Foucault had been doing well at school, his performance suddenly fell off and he did very badly in his end-of-year examinations in the summer of 1940. To his dismay and surprise, he was told he would have to re-sit them. His brother has suggested that a newly arrived teacher took an immediate personal dislike to Paul-Michel and even began to mark his work unfairly. It has also been suggested that the boy was overawed by the arrival of much more sophisticated pupils from the Lycée Janson-de-Sailly, which had been evacuated from Paris, and could not compete with them. Furious at what she perceived as the unfair treatment of her son, Mme Foucault removed him from the *lycée* and enrolled him at the Collège Saint-Stanislas (inevitably know as 'Saint-Stan'). This was a religious establishment run by the Frères des Ecoles Chrétiennes, also known as the Frères Chrétiens (and, less flatteringly, as the Frères Ignorantins). The school did not enjoy the same status as the local Jesuit College, but it had a fairly good reputation. Mme Foucault believed that it would provide a more stable environment than a state school, because priests and lay brothers working in the private religious school sector were not liable to military call up. She was mistaken. Paul-Michel entered *terminale* (roughly equivalent to an English sixth form) in 1942, only to learn that Canon Duret, who should have been his philosophy teacher, had been arrested and deported to Germany because of his involvement in the local resistance. Even before his arrest, he had displayed his hostility to the new regime by insisting, at considerable risk to himself, that the portrait of Pétain displayed in his classroom had to be hung below the crucifix and not above it as regulations demanded.

The replacement appointed by the school was a literature specialist. Mme Foucault believed that philosophy should be taught by philosophers and protested loudly that this was not good enough. A new teacher was found at Ligugé. The Benedictine Dom Perrot has been described as an erudite but dogmatic Thomist who was hostile to modern philosophy from Descartes onwards. Shortly before Perrot actually took up his post, Mme Foucault resorted to the classic solution of looking for a private tutor for her son and went to ask the dean of the University's Faculty of Arts for advice. As a result of this conversation, the 20-year-old Louis Girard came to the rue Arthur Ranc on Thursdays to teach Paul-Michel philosophy. As Girard had yet to take his own degree in philosophy, he could do little more than regurgitate the watered-down version of Kant he was studying. Even so, he believed that his 'pupil' did learn something and, like so many people, was greatly impressed by his capacity for work. The arrangement lasted for little more than a year. Girard was conscripted for work in Germany in August 1943.

The philosophy courses that Foucault followed at school were designed to supply pupils with a broad knowledge of the subject rather than to initiate them into its technical intricacies. The subject was subdivided into the sub-categories of psychology, logic and ethics. Teaching was based upon a list of texts approved by the Ministry of Education, and the list varied very little from year to year. Philosophy began with the Greeks but pride of place went to the seventeenth and eighteenth centuries, as represented by

Descartes, Pascal, Leibniz, Kant, Spinoza, Rousseau and Condillac. Although Claude Bernard and Auguste Comte did figure in the syllabus, few teachers ventured very far into even the nineteenth century and, for philosophical purposes, the twentieth did not yet exist.

Having passed his *bac* in June 1943, Foucault was automatically qualified to go to university, but his plans and ambitions were changing. He now wished to go on studying philosophy, and was intent on going to the elite Ecole Normale Supérieure in Paris. This meant studying for the difficult competitive entrance exam or *concours*. 'Saint-Stan' did not have the staff or the resources to teach for the *concours,* and Foucault returned to his old *lycée*. He was attempting the impossible. Even though the standard of teaching at Henri-IV was good, it was notoriously difficult for anyone in a provincial school to get into ENS, which recruited mainly from a handful of elite schools in Paris. Almost predictably, but much to the surprise of his fellow students, Foucault narrowly failed the oral part of the *concours* in the spring of 1945, and was therefore inadmissible for the written papers.

As the war lurched to an end, there were further upheavals. The family moved out of their house temporarily. The rue Arthur Ranc was near the railway station, which was an obvious target for Allied bombers. Dr Foucault and his wife moved into rented accommodation in town, while the children were sent to Le Piroir. This proved to be a wise decision, because the garage attached to the house was destroyed during an air raid on 13 June 1944. The arrival of peace meant that Foucault could now improve his chances of getting into ENS by going to study in Paris. While this was in some ways an obvious strategy, it was not without its difficulties. In theory, French *lycées* recruit their pupils from geographically defined catchment areas. In practice, there have always been ways around this. A surprising number of families eager to send their children to particular schools suddenly discover that they have relatives in the catchment area and that they can use their addresses. Precisely how Paul-Michel Foucault qualified for admission to the Lycée Henri-IV is not clear, but it is almost certain that his mother had a hand in it. This might explain the peculiar living arrangements that were made for him. Although Henri-IV took boarders, Foucault was not one of them. He lived for a year in a room in a private school run by a friend of his mother's.

It was not the best moment for anyone to go to live in Paris. Food rationing was still in force. There was a severe housing shortage. Industrial unrest was worsening, especially in the northern coal basins. The transport system was still in chaos and travel was difficult. The first post-war winters were exceptionally harsh and all fuel was in short supply. Foucault's first year in Paris cannot have been easy. He was alone for the first time and, although he often complained, not without justification, that he came from a stifling provincial background, he had until now led a very sheltered life in a very safe and protective family. He rarely spoke of this period in his life, but a year spent in the *khâgne* that prepares candidates for the *concours* is rarely a pleasant experience. It is an endless round of lessons, revision and mock examinations, and has only one purpose: passing the *concours.* That Foucault survived his year of isolation is testimony to his almost stoic ability to tolerate loneliness and to his self-sufficiency.

The Lycée Henri-IV is in the rue Clovis, immediately behind the Panthéon. It is a somewhat forbidding building. Its walls are almost blank façades relieved only by rows of narrow windows. The single entrance gives on to an internal recreation yard with drab rows of pollarded trees. The building itself is a labyrinth of long corridors and stone stairways. Although classes were large – up to 50 – the teaching was of a very high standard. Foucault was taught history by André Alba, a man noted for both his erudition and his anti-clerical republicanism, and philosophy by Jean Hyppolite. His first encounter with Hyppolite lasted for only

The entrance to Lycee Henri-IV, Paris.

two months, as the philosopher then left to take up a post at the University of Strasbourg, but it marked him for life. Hyppolite was perhaps the greatest of the Hegelians who totally changed the face of post-war philosophy in France. He was also a remarkable orator and public speaker. Listening to him in the classroom was, Foucault would recall, like listening to Hegel himself, or even to the voice of philosophy.[7] He was in fact listening to a very early oral version of the major study of Hegel's *Phenomenology of Mind* (which Hyppolite had already translated), which would appear in 1959. The year at Henri-IV had the desired effect. When he re-sat the *concours*, Foucault was ranked fourth in the country. It seems almost improbably symbolic, but the oral examination represented his first encounter with a man who was to become a good friend and to have an enormous influence on his work and career: Georges Canguilhem, schools inspector for philosophy and professor of the history and philosophy of the sciences at the University of Strasbourg. Canguilhem remembered nothing of this first meeting. Foucault was merely another candidate to be examined.

Foucault came from precisely the kind of background that so many young people rebelled against. His personal revolt took two forms. He hated being called 'Paul-Michel' and always referred to himself simply as 'Michel', even though he remained 'Paul-Michel' for official and administrative purposes. Perhaps this was a rebellion against a father many describe as brusque and authoritarian, but both his brother and his sister offer an alternative interpretation. In the playground 'Paul-Michel' was easily corrupted into 'Polichinelle', the French equivalent to Punchinello, and that could become the basis for jokes about *le secret de Polichinelle* (an open secret). As an adult, Foucault could be very prickly; even as a child, he did not take kindly to being teased. The second form of rebellion was more serious. At the precocious age of ten, he announced that he would not follow the family tradition and would not become a doctor: he was going to be a history teacher. Relations with his family and with his father in particular deteriorated badly. His refusal to become a doctor should in fact have come as no surprise, since the boy had never shown any interest in or aptitude for the natural sciences.

There is a persistent rumour, which it is now impossible to confirm or deny, that it was in fact his father who made him allergic to medicine by insisting that he attend an amputation 'to make a man of him'. The experience sickened him. The anecdote is not implausible because Paul Foucault did seem to savour the macabre. He once took the surrealist painter André Masson, whom he had met through a mutual acquaintance and who became his patient, to see the corpse of a child with a curious lesion that exposed parts of the brain membrane. Masson was inspired to make a sinister whirling drawing which he gave to his doctor. For years it hung on the wall of Michel Foucault's study and is now in the possession of his brother. The young Foucault also had something of a liking for the macabre aspects of medicine. On at least one occasion he cycled out to the Institut de Larnay on the outskirts of Poitiers. Founded in the mid-nineteenth century, the Institut, which still exists in a rather different form, was run by nuns and attempted to care for the deaf-mute women they described as 'souls in prison'. Its most famous inmate was Marthe Heurtin, who was blind as well as deaf and dumb. After a very difficult early life, she was taken into the Institute in 1910 and taught by the nuns to establish at least some communication with others. Although the Institut de Larnay was, for its day, a progressive and even pioneering establishment, it still clung to some of the more repellent customs of the previous century, and Heurtin was sometimes on display to the public. Foucault was, according to his brother, quite fascinated by her.

Whatever the truth or otherwise of the amputation anecdote, it was always notoriously difficult to persuade the adult Foucault to consult a doctor. Although his relationship with his father was strained, there was no actual break between them. Foucault's parents expected their children to succeed, and they rewarded success. Asked what he would like as a reward for passing the *concours*, Paul-Michel immediately asked for German lessons. He had studied Greek, Latin and English at school, but not German. In his oral, he had been criticized for mispronouncing a word from a language he did not speak and he was determined that it would not happen again. A German tutor was found for him.

Foucault left home in 1946 to attend a *lycée* in Paris and rarely returned to Poitiers until his father died in 1959, not least because he was working and living abroad for much of the time. After that date, he always devoted his Augusts to his mother. When her husband died she retreated to Le Piroir to live with Foucault's grandmother (who died in July 1961), and had central heating installed to overcome the damp problem. A study and an almost monastic bedroom were permanently reserved for Michel in what had once been the servants' quarters. The study was sparsely furnished, but it was a good place to revise manuscripts and to correct proofs. Foucault's visits to Le Piroir always coincided with the gherkin harvest and one of his self-appointed tasks was to scrub the little vegetables before pickling them in vinegar to make the year's supply of *cornichons*. Watering the garden was a daily ritual, and carrying heavy watering cans an improvised form of weight-lifting. Foucault often spoke bitterly of his childhood and the provincial bourgeoisie in which he grew up, but he always had some affection for the region. As he was dying from AIDS-related complaints in 1984, he was still making plans to purchase a rambling old vicarage in the nearby hamlet of La Verrue.

Despite their evident differences, Foucault did in some ways identify with his father. He often described himself as a 'diagnostician' and his work as a diagnosis of the present rather than a bearer of timeless truths. The 'diagnosis' image derives, as he admitted, from Nietzsche, but he also remarked that, when he wrote, he was tracing on paper the same aggressive signs that his father once traced on the body when he operated: 'I've transformed the scalpel into a penholder.'[8] The scalpel image actually provides a very accurate picture of how Foucault worked. He did not so much read books as dissect them, harvesting quotations in the way that organs are harvested for transplant and grafting them on to his own texts.

Foucault was usually very reticent about his childhood and rarely related it to his work. Like Nietzsche, he usually took the view that 'I am one thing, my writings are another',[9] and almost never spoke of his subjective life. In an interview given in 1967, he did, however, confide that he had always been troubled by a nightmare of looking at a text he could not read. He could decipher only a tiny proportion of it, but went on pretending to read it even though he knew that he was making it up as he went along. Suddenly, the whole text became blurred and he could no longer read it at all. At that point, his throat felt constricted and he woke up. He never offered any interpretation of his nightmare.[10]

If little is known about the subjective life of the young Foucault, even less is known about his sexuality. In 1981 he did state that he had always desired boys and had always wanted sexual relations with boys, adding that he did not find his first 'friend' until he was twenty.[11] The friend has never been identified, but the encounter must have taken place in Paris. Whether or not he had any previous sexual experience is a matter for speculation, but pre-war Poitiers was scarcely the place for experimentation and there was little private space in Foucault's life. His conversations with Louis Girard were not punctuated by personal confidences, and his tutor had no insight into his pupil's orientation. The two kept in touch after the war and when he was preparing for his own marriage in 1947, Girard joked 'Your turn next'. Foucault blushed, and Girard suddenly 'realized'. It was also dangerous to be homosexual in occupied France. In August 1942 Amendment 334 was added to the Penal Code. The age of consent was raised to 21, and sex with a minor of the same sex became punishable by imprisonment for between six months and three years, and fines of between 2,000 and 6,000 francs. Minors indulging in consensual sex could be prosecuted for 'mutual aggravated assault'. This was the first homophobic legislation to be adopted since the offence of sodomy was removed from the statute book during the Revolution. Article 334 was in keeping with Vichy's emphasis on 'family values', but it also reflected the conviction that the Third Republic lost the war because it had been undermined from within by a culture of effeminacy, decadence and, at least by implication, homosexuality.

Immediately before leaving for Paris, Foucault had a significant encounter. Jean Piel was a man for whom the expression 'networking' might have been coined and one who existed at the point where different worlds intersected. Born in either 1901 or 1902 (he always refused to say which), he had studied both philosophy and political economy, but never had an academic career. He was as at home in ministerial corridors as he was in literary salons. He was married to Simone Maklès, who was one of three sisters. Rose Maklès married the Surrealist painter André Masson, while Sylvia was married first to Georges Bataille and then to Jacques Lacan. Piel was therefore close to the centre of what would become a new post-war avant-garde. He was a mediator, little known to the general public but extremely influential behind the scenes of intellectual life.

Piel had been taken prisoner in 1940, but in 1946 he was appointed Secretary General for Economic Affairs and was posted to Poitiers, where it was his task to re-establish the transport and telecommunications systems and to revitalize agriculture. It is a measure of just how far the Foucault family connections extended that Piel already knew them vaguely. While he was based in Poitiers, Piel had a car accident and was operated on by Dr Foucault. The operation was not entirely successful and left him with a bad limp that greatly reduced his mobility. Piel had little direct contact with Foucault himself at this time, but he certainly noticed him and later kept an eye on his progress from afar.

Although he never again lived permanently in Poitiers and usually spoke disparagingly of his bourgeois origins, Foucault remained marked by both his place of birth and the values of his family. His years at *lycée* gave him the precious asset of the easy familiarity with classical French culture that is so important in social terms. The serious and hard-working schoolboy grew up to be a man for whom intellectual work was all-important: coming from Foucault '*ça, c'est du travail*' ('now that's work') was high praise indeed. His family inculcated certain social skills into him and, although he suffered bouts of depression and attacks of shyness, he was rarely ill at ease in company and was always able to mix with an extraordinary variety of people. He was a good and attentive host. He was from a privileged background that he took for granted and it gave him many valuable social skills as well as confidence. He accepted honours and privileges easily and almost as though they were his by right.

In the world of the provincial bourgeoisie, wealth was certainly important but flaunting it was regarded as being in poor taste. Bourgeois homes were, by contemporary standards, heavily furnished and over-decorated, but ostentatiously vulgar luxury and conspicuous consumption were frowned upon. Foucault was never poor and became rich on a good salary, book royalties and fees for lecture tours. Yet he never made any attempt to display his wealth. He usually dressed very simply, even carelessly. To his amusement, a Canadian interviewer expressed surprise at seeing such a distinguished professor wandering around the campus of Toronto University dressed in jeans, a white tee-shirt and a black leather jacket.[12] The interviewer probably did not realize that this apparel was, at least in Paris, a recognizably gay uniform. The various apartments Foucault lived in were certainly comfortable and well furnished, but they were also bare to the point of starkness, rather as though he always followed the bourgeois principle of *acheter peu, mais acheter cher* ('Buy little but buy expensive'). The apartment in the rue de Vaugirard, where he lived from 1970 until his death in 1984, was decorated in a stark modernist style, with very few ornaments. He worked at a table of steel and glass. For most of his adult life, Foucault lived and worked in an almost monochrome home environment, and it is perhaps significant that his occasional writings on painting (in which he took a serious interest) contain so little discussion of colour. For the provincial bourgeoisie, money was something to be accumulated, but it was not something to be talked about. Foucault could be very generous and often donated large sums of money to political and other causes, but the donations were made with such discretion as to make them almost anonymous. There was always something of the discreet charm of the bourgeoisie about Michel Foucault.

Two

Founded in 1794, the Ecole Normale Supérieure is one of France's *grandes écoles* or elite schools. Its remit has always been to ensure that the country's best young minds are taught by the best teachers. A student who enters it at 20 can reasonably expect to take a first degree in one or two years, and the *agrégation* at the end of three years. France's highest competitive examination, the *agrég* is the passport to an academic or equivalent career. Foucault's contemporaries and near-contemporaries were a representative sample. Robert Mauzi, who was a year younger than Foucault, became a distinguished specialist in eighteenth-century French literature. Jean Laplanche and Didier Anzieu went on to become very eminent psychoanalysts. Alan Peyrefitte went into the diplomatic service and then enjoyed a ministerial career, while Paul Villaneix became the biographer of the historian Michelet. Foucault's friend Maurice Pinguet spent most of his career as director of the Maison de France in Tokyo and became a respected Orientalist. ENS provided an apprenticeship in knowledge, but it also supplied an entry into a world where politics, philosophy and literature intersected.

Foucault had entered an all-male residential institution. It was self-contained and had its own excellent library. Like all *normaliens*, Foucault was very conscious of being at an elite institution that was vastly superior to the lowly Sorbonne, even though he attended lectures there. The sense of being part of an elite was reinforced by the affected use of an impenetrable jargon in which

The entrance to the Ecole Normale Supérieure, Paris.

a third-year student was known as a *cube*, and alumni as *archicubes*.
Great emphasis was placed on *l'esprit normalien* and the need to
briller ('to shine', 'to be brilliant'), especially in oral examinations.
For sceptics, the mandarin *esprit normalien* means the ability to

speak or write at length about almost topic without actually saying anything. The hot-house atmosphere of the school traditionally combines a strong sense of institutional identity and *esprit de corps* with a very high level of individual competitiveness.

The school was a closely knit community, though arts and science students tended to keep apart. Although Foucault and his fellow *normaliens* worked hard, they also indulged in horseplay and kept up the long-standing tradition of dropping water bombs down stairwells. The school was far from luxurious or even comfortable. The old building in the rue d'Ulm was sadly in need of renovation. Students slept in draughty dormitories partitioned by curtains. Meals were taken collectively in the refectory and the cuisine was not noted for its excellence.

In a relatively small institution such as this, the role of individual teachers is vital, and it is quite usual for an *archicube* to describe a particularly influential teacher as his *maître* or 'master'. In Foucault's case, the master was Louis Althusser, the school's philosophy tutor or *caiman*. Born in 1918, Althusser was still making the transition from Catholicism to Marxism and was unknown to anyone outside the rue d'Ulm. He neither sought nor obtained high office in the Party. Althusser was never a very public man, but his intellectual rigour and skills as a teacher – he was often consulted by students revising for the last year of the *agrég* – meant that he had a great impact on the small groups he taught. He suffered from serious mental health problems, which were eventually diagnosed as resulting from manic depression, and regularly spent periods in the school's sanatorium. His periodic stays in psychiatric hospitals were, for official purposes, short holidays.

Like Althusser, Foucault had his demons. He did not really take to institutional life. He did join in the horseplay and the fights with wet towels, but there was a darker side to his life at ENS. There are rumours of self-harming incidents and suicide attempts. There were serious and repeated bouts of depression. While ENS did have a culture in which almost every student had and cultivated his neurosis, things were more serious in Foucault's case. He was drinking heavily. Some acquaintances hint that he was using drugs too. His drug use probably involved nothing harder than cannabis, which was readily available to anyone bold enough to stray into the Arab cafés in the rue Xavier-Privas in the Latin Quarter. The underlying cause of Foucault's depression was, it is widely accepted, his difficulty in coming to terms with his homosexuality.

Discussing Herculine Barbin, the eighteenth-century hermaphrodite whose memoirs he published in 1978, Foucault wrote in a gay magazine of the 'happy non-identity' of life in closed societies, 'both closed and warm', and of 'the strange happiness, at once obligatory and forbidden, of knowing only one sex'.[1] Herculine spent her early life in a religious and almost exclusively female world. Eventually recognized as being a 'real boy', she / he could not adapt and committed suicide. Foucault may have desired it, but he did not discover that strange happiness in the all-male environment of ENS or in post-war Paris. This was neither the time nor the place to be a young and uncertain homosexual. There were, as yet, no 'gay' organizations. The Vichy law on the age of consent was still on the statute book and it was well known that the police kept unofficial files on gay men. Sex was certainly available, but only in secret. The Tuileries gardens were still the sexual playground they had been ever since the seventeenth century. Certain of the cast-iron urinals that were a feature of the street furniture of Paris until the early 1970s were well-known pick-up spots, dubbed *tasses* ('cups'). Partners could readily be found in a few bars in Montparnasse and Pigalle and under some of the bridges over the Seine, particularly if the seeker wanted rough trade and dared to go to the Pont de Clichy. Foucault would sometimes simply disappear and return days later, looking exhausted, hung over and dishevelled. The most likely explanation was that he had disappeared on some sexual escapade.

Whether he knew it or not, Foucault was under observation. At his mother's request, Jacqueline Verdeaux, now practising as a psychiatrist, was keeping a watchful eye on him and reporting back to Poitiers. Foucault was eventually persuaded to consult Jean Delay at the Sainte-Anne hospital. Born in 1907, Delay was one of the most distinguished psychiatrists of his day. He had written extensively on virtually every aspect of his specialism and enjoyed the reputation of being an excellent administrator. One of the pioneers of the use of neuroleptics and psychotropes in psychiatry, he was also a writer and the author of a psychobiography of André Gide that is still highly regarded. He also had something in common with Foucault: his father was a surgeon who had expected him to take up the same career. His choice of psychiatry had been his form of rebellion. Precisely what happened between Foucault and Delay is not on record, but it did result in a lasting friendship and exchanges of their respective books. It also had a more concrete outcome. With the consent of ENS's doctor Pierre Etienne, Foucault spent his third and final year in the relative comfort of a single room in the sanatorium. A further attempt to cure the depression was made when Foucault went into psychoanalysis. It did not last.

Not everyone who knew Foucault at this time met a depressive. His sister, now married and living in Paris, was in regular contact with him and usually found him cheerful. Pinguet recalled encountering a Foucault dressed in shorts who addressed those around him in loud, almost aggressive terms, but saw nothing untoward about him. It was only later that he learned from Foucault himself that his years at ENS had been almost unbearably painful.[2] These differing perceptions are not necessarily contradictory. Foucault always had a talent for living several lives at the same time, and for appearing different to different people. Some found him a pleasant companion; others encountered a Foucault who could use his considerable rhetorical skills as lethal weapons and who refused to admit defeat in arguments.

Academically, Foucault performed well, taking a degree in philosophy in 1948 and a degree in psychology the following year. Widely regarded by his fellow students as brilliant, his appetite for work was famous, but he now reverted to the pattern established at his *lycée* by unexpectedly failing his *agrégation* in 1950. This time, no special arrangements could be made and he had to prepare for a re-sit. For much of the year, he revised intensively with Jean-Paul Aron, a friend from the Sorbonne. Both were homosexual and both had an acid sense of humour.

The intensive revision paid off and Foucault was successful in his second attempt to pass the *agrég*. The written papers were on 'experience and theory', and candidates were also required to write an imaginary dialogue between Bergson and Spinoza. It was the oral that produced the shock. In accordance with established tradition, candidates were required to take a sheet of paper from a basket and then improvise on the theme it gave them. To Foucault's outrage, his topic was 'sexuality'. In his view, that was not an appropriate subject and he protested loudly. The topic had never been set before but had been introduced by Canguilhem, who argued that it was a perfectly suitable topic: students talked about it all the time. The exchange was a reminder that the austere and bad-tempered historian of science did have a sense of humour. This was a man who, with deliberate malice, would address any nun who crossed his path as *madame* and not, as was the norm, as *ma soeur*. There was nothing humorous about Canguilhem's notorious temper, but he usually reserved his anger for colleagues he deemed 'incompetent' and did not direct it at his students. As some knew to their cost, it was inadvisable to appear incompetent in Canguilhem's eyes: his anger could destroy careers.

Canguilhem had succeeded Gaston Bachelard as the Sorbonne's Professor of the History of Science. His work was not widely known outside specialist circles and his only major publication to date was his thesis of 1943 on 'the normal and the pathological'. Given that his reputation and influence were so great, it is always difficult to come to terms with the fact that Canguilhem, who died in 1995, published relatively little, and that almost all his publications were short essays that he modestly described 'traces of a trade'. Most of his work deals with the history of medicine and the life sciences. For Canguilhem, the history of a science – he inevitably speaks of *sciences* in the plural, and never of an abstract and monolithic *science* – is not a record of smooth and cumulative process. It is discontinuous and punctuated by what his predecessor Bachelard called epistemological breaks. A science begins to emerge when it breaks with its pre-scientific past and rejects it as ideological. Epistemological breaks, which can in some respects be likened to Kuhn's paradigm shifts, are not brought about by empirical discoveries but by conceptual displacements. The introduction of the concept of 'fever', for example, does not reflect the discovery of an empirical disease, but the break that occurs when medical thought is no longer governed by pre-scientific categories such as 'miasma' and is reorganized around new ways of conceiving the body, the vectors that transmit fevers and the role of doctors. To that extent, the history of a science is that of the errors it has detected and overcome in its own past.[3]

In the year that he failed his *agrég*, Foucault became a member of the Parti Communiste Française (PCF). This was the only time that he joined a political party; in the 1970s he would be very active on a variety of political fronts, but never as a member of a party. Like many other young people at the time, he saw the PCF and Communism as offering an alternative to the dangerously threatening world constructed for them by their parents' generation. The news that Paul-Michel had become a Communist caused something of a scandal back home in Poitiers: refusing to train as a doctor was bad enough, but joining the PCF was infinitely worse.

Foucault does not appear to have been a very good Communist. Maurice Pinguet, for instance, had no recollection of him taking much part in the weekly cell meetings held in a café in the place de la Contrescarpe.[4] While he began to teach part-time at ENS, Foucault was associated with a group of slightly younger Party members, including the historian Paul Veyne, the literary theorist Gérard Genette, Pinguet and the sociologist Jean-Claude Passeron. Veyne recalls that they were regarded by the Party hierarchy as 'future heretics', and it is true that they did all resign their membership. Foucault himself resigned over the so-called doctors' plot of 1953. At the beginning of the year, nine doctors were arrested and charged with planning to murder a number of Soviet marshals and of plotting against Stalin himself. Stalin died – of purely natural causes – on 3 March, and the Soviet press almost immediately announced that the doctors, now described as the victims of 'a machination', had been released. Seven of the nine doctors were Jewish, and the affair revealed an ugly strand of anti-Semitism in both the Soviet Union and the ever-loyal PCF.

Anti-Semitism was not the only thing that made the PCF an uncomfortable place to be: 'I was never really integrated into the Communist Party because I was homosexual, and it was an institution that reinforced all the values of the most traditional bourgeois life.'[5] In his memoirs, the historian Leroy Ladurie, also a youthful Party member at this time, recalls the incident in which a schoolteacher was forced to resign his position when it was discovered – or at least alleged – that he had made sexual overtures to a student. He was also forced out of a Party that believed that 'one Party member's homosexual pollution would infect the whole of the Communist collectivity'.[6] The Party believed firmly in marriage, the family and 'proletarian' morality. Being a Communist homosexual, or a homosexual Communist, was not an option.

As he neared the end of his course, Foucault became liable for military service. Deferments were available for those in full-time education, but he could not hope to be granted a further reprieve. Avoiding national service was, like contriving to gain admission to elite schools, something of a sport for the French middle classes. Foucault failed his medical and was declared unfit for service. According to his partner Daniel Defert, he had learned in advance what the eye tests would be and deliberately failed them. Coming from a medical family and being a student of psychology, it cannot have been difficult to acquire the required knowledge. Foucault's brother was never a soldier either.

Foucault had successfully avoided doing his military service but now had to avoid a further ordeal. In the highly centralized French system, movement between the secondary and higher sectors was common, and it was the norm for graduates and *agrégés* to teach in a *lycée* for two years before taking up university posts or going into research. Once more, Foucault found a way to avoid the inevitable. In June 1951 he applied for and was awarded a scholarship to the Fondation Thiers, a research foundation housed in a sumptuous *hôtel particulier* in the sixteenth *arrondissement.* This was another all-male residential institution and Foucault again found it difficult to settle. He left before the end of his first year, even though he had been awarded a scholarship for three years, and abandoned the thesis he had planned to write on the post-Cartesians and the birth of psychology.

Foucault was certainly ambitious and highly competitive, but his ambition was surprisingly unfocused and he was still uncertain about his future. Although he had studied philosophy, he was increasingly fascinated by psychology and psychiatry, and was awarded a diploma in psychopathology in the summer of 1952 after studying with Jean Delay at the Institut de Psychologie. He now began to acquire at least some practical experience of the world of psychiatry and the fields that would be the focus of his work over the coming decades. That experience was mainly gained at Sainte-Anne.

Sainte-Anne was originally a 'clinical asylum' for the treatment of the mentally ill. Building began in 1863 and the asylum was completed six years later. The western and larger section consisted of twelve wards built in a quadrilateral; the eastern section housed the administrative building and two wards for difficult patients. The whole complex was surrounded by a high wall pierced by only two gates. In early 1950s the hospital's original layout was still recognizable, but it now contained an excellent medical library and rich archives, and the institution was now also a teaching hospital. Sainte-Anne is only a short walk away from another building behind a high wall. This is La Santé prison, which was built in 1867. Throughout his work, Foucault stresses that there is a close connection between prisons and psychiatric hospitals, and Sainte-Anne and La Santé do look ominously similar.

It was Jacqueline Verdeaux who arranged for Foucault to work at Sainte-Anne. She and her husband were running an electro-encephalography unit established at the request of Delay, described by Foucault as the man who 'introduced me to the world of the mad'.[7] Foucault had little more than observer status, although he was involved in making diagnostic tests and carrying out experiments. His qualifications in psychiatry were academic rather than clinical. He had followed lecture courses given by Daniel Lagache and then a series of lectures by Daumézon on institutional psychotherapy at ENS. He had attended the *présentation des malades* at Sainte-Anne. The *présentation* was a curious rite in which patients were examined in front of an audience of students, and served both as a diagnostic tool and a teaching device. Thanks to Jacqueline Verdeaux's personal influence, Foucault was also able to work as her unofficial assistant at the Centre d'Orientation at Fresnes prison, just outside Paris. Fresnes was the headquarters of the prison medical service, and the Centre's role was to draw up psychiatric reports on prisoners who had just entered the system. Their function was to determine suicide risks and to determine whether individual prisoners would benefit from being sent to any particular institutions.

To make any further progress, Foucault would have had to acquire medical or at least clinical qualifications, and he was reluctant to do so. It would have been an interesting time to go into psychiatry, since the post-war years were a period of innovation and reform. The impetus behind the reform movement was a feeling of shame: patients in French psychiatric institutions had died in their tens of thousands during the Occupation, mainly as a result of neglect and malnutrition. It was in the late 1940s and the 1950s that new forms of theory began to be developed and that the old notion of the asylum began to give way to that of the therapeutic community. Psychoanalysis was at last becoming an established form of therapy after years of derision and hostility on the part of the medical establishment. In *Histoire de la folie* Foucault describes the origins of the medical-carceral psychiatric hospital; he could have been one of those who sought to reform and humanize it.

Jacqueline Verdeaux had become very interested in the work of the Swiss psychiatrist Ludwig Binswanger (1881–1966) and was struggling to translate his *Traum und Existenz*, first published in 1930. She needed help with some of the specialist terminology, and turned to Foucault, whose German – largely self-taught – was now good enough for him to read Heidegger and Husserl in the original. He readily agreed to help as best he could. She then asked him to write an introduction. Foucault plunged into Binswanger. The introduction he finally produced was twice the length of the text it was supposed to be presenting. Binswanger was almost unknown in Paris, and no one outside ENS knew who Foucault was. It was, not surprisingly, only with considerable difficulty that Verdeaux found a publisher for the text in 1954, and it was not a success.[8]

Just before Lent 1952, Foucault went with the Verdeaux to visit a clinic on the shores on Lake Constance in Sweden. It was run by Binswanger's follower Roland Kuhn and was the scene of a curious yearly ritual. The inmates spent much of the spring making large and elaborate masks for themselves and the staff. On Shrove Tuesday they processed through the neighbouring town of Musterlingen, led by a giant figure representing Carnival. Staff and patients were all masked, and were therefore indistinguishable from one another. When they returned to the hospital grounds, the masks were taken off and the Carnival figure was burned with great ceremony. Georges Verdeaux filmed the procession for research purposes and there is something very eerie about his silent home movie. Foucault's *Histoire de la folie* describes the Ship of Fools gliding along the rivers and canals of northern Europe; it could well have begun with a description of a carnival in Switzerland.

A second commission soon came along. During his last years at Lyon's Lycée du Parc, Althusser had been taught by Jean Lacroix. Lacroix (1900–1986) was a Catholic with a background in classical philosophy, but he was also open-minded enough to take a close interest in developments within contemporary thought. From its launch in late 1944 to December 1980, Lacroix published a column in the daily *Le Monde*, which must have been the first newspaper in the world to have a regular philosophy correspondent. At Althusser's suggestion, he commissioned Foucault to write a short book on mental illness for the 'Initiation Philosophique' collection he edited for Presses Universitaires de France (PUF).

Foucault repeatedly describes French philosophy as being structured around a dichotomy between a philosophy of subjectivity and a philosophy of concepts and locates his own work within the latter tradition.[9] 'Subjectivity' refers primarily to the phenomenological tradition, and to Sartre in particular; concepts, to the school of epistemology associated with Bachelard, Canguilhem and Althusser. While this is a not inaccurate, if rather schematic, description, it applies to the mid-1960s rather than the 1950s, when the field of philosophy was organized around Marxism and various forms of phenomenology and existentialism. The other dominant influence was the new Hegelianism of men like Hyppolite. While Foucault respected and admired Hyppolite, he was also distrustful of any totalizing philosophy that promised the cumulative acquisition of total knowledge or understanding. Phenomenology, in contrast, was an attempt to construct a rigorous knowledge of specific objects, and especially consciousness, on the basis of strict descriptions of how they are experienced. Foucault's earliest works are influenced by both phenomenology and Marxism. He never again refers to these early writings, and did not want them to be republished. When PUF insisted on reprinting *Maladie mentale* in 1962 he rewrote the second half, expunging any trace of the Marxism he had imbibed during his time in the PCF and replacing it with what is effectively a very condensed version of *Histoire de la folie*.[10]

Binswanger and Kuhn developed a form of therapy known as *Daseinanalyse* which draws heavily upon Heidegger's phenomenology: *Dasein* (literally 'being-there') is the philosopher's term for human existence or man's being in the world. Mental illness is viewed by Binswanger and Khun as a specific mode of existing in the world, and dreams are described as the main expression of that mode of being. Whereas Freudian analysis typically regards dreams as expressions of repressed wishes, *Daseinanalyse* sees them as actual experiences. The feeling of 'standing too close to the edge', which is a common symptom of depression, is not symbolic: the patient is, in terms of his or her inner life, in real danger of falling. For the Foucault who wrote *Maladie mentale*, this form of analysis allows the clinician to move away from the old system in which individual experiences are forced into diagnostic categories such as hysteria or schizophrenia, which seem to exist as abstract entities that have nothing to do with individual experience and suffering. He combines this account of *Daseinanalyse* with references to economic and personal alienation and to the 'real conditions' that induce mental illness which clearly derive from the rather mechanistic Marxism of his student years, as to the glowing (and subsequently embarrassing) references to Pavlovian psychology. It is also tempting to read *Maladie mentale* as a very personal document. It contains frequent references to *angoisse*, which is equivalent to the English 'anxiety' and 'anguish' as well as to the German *Angst*, and to suicidal tendencies. Foucault also insists that, popular wisdom notwithstanding, anyone suffering from mental illness is well aware of that fact and does not live in a state of blissful ignorance. Mental illness implies, that is, a form of 'ill-consciousness' or an existential sense of being ill. While it would probably be a mistake to place too much emphasis on psychological explanations that can be no more than speculative, the author was a young man with considerable personal experience of depression.

After leaving the Fondation Thiers, Foucault shared an apartment in the rue Monge with his brother, who was now well on his way to becoming the family's next Dr Foucault. The rue Monge was convenient for ENS, but that was no longer Foucault's primary place of work. He had found an assistantship in the northern city of Lille, where Raymond Polin, who was head of the university's philosophy department, was looking for someone to teach the psychology part of the degree course. Foucault's name had been mentioned to him by Jules Vuillemin, friend of Louis Althusser and professor of philosophy at Clermont-Ferrand. He had also met Foucault, albeit only briefly. Foucault chose not to live in Lille, at the time a grim industrial city of textile and jute mills. In continuing to live in Paris while working elsewhere, he was conforming to a recognizable pattern. Poor research and library facilities outside the capital meant that many academics were reluctant to move away from it, and they commuted to their work in provincial universities whenever possible. Foucault crammed his teaching and contact hours into as short a time as possible, and travelled the 200 kilometres to Lille by train, staying overnight in a hotel only when it was essential to do so. He had personal as well as intellectual reasons for remaining in Paris, because he was now involved in an intense relationship with a young musician and composer.

Born in 1928, Jean Barraqué had been educated at Notre Dame's choir school and then at the Lycée Condorcet. His passion for music was total and he seemed to have little interest in anything else. In the early 1950s he began to attend classes in counterpoint, fugue and harmony at the Conservatoire, even though he was not officially enrolled as a student. He also attended the 'analysis' course taught by the great organist and composer Olivier Messiaen. Barraqué had long been fascinated by the Romantic school and Debussy, but he was now discovering Webern and the second Viennese school, as well as the early work of Stockhausen. By 1951 he had become involved with Pierre Schaefer's experiments in *musique concrète* – an early version of electronic music and music for tape. In 1952 he completed his *Sonata for Piano*, which was his first major opus.

Foucault and Barraqué met at Royaumont in the summer of 1952. A former Cistercian abbey just to the north of Paris, Royaumont had been used as a cultural centre since 1936, and Althusser often took reading parties of students there to revise for their *agrégation* orals. Foucault and Aron had been there for that purpose in 1950. The two went there again in 1952, and their short stay coincided with that of a group of musicians organized by Pierre Boulez.[11] The group was Domaine musical and its self-appointed mission was to bring together and promote all the post-Weberian tendencies in European music. A year older than Foucault, Boulez was the musical director for the Renaud-Barrault theatre company, but early compositions such as the *Sonatine* for flute and piano (1946) and the piano sonatas of 1946 and 1948 had already revealed the talent that would make him one of Europe's most important composers. Thanks to his relationship with Barraqué, Foucault regularly met the group of musicians and composers associated with Boulez. They usually went for a drink together; Barraqué's fondness for *un petit vin blanc* was well known to all.

When he met Foucault, Barraqué was making a precarious living by writing programme notes for concerts and giving private lessons. He was also working on a composition he first called *Three Songs*. His original intention was to use lyrics borrowed from the

Song of Songs and poems by Baudelaire and Rimbaud. The composition was reworked again and again, and finally became *Séquence* (1950–55), a 20-minute piece scored for voice, percussion and instrumental ensemble. In its final version, which was premiered in March 1956, the lyrics come from the lament in the 'Sorcerer' section of *Also Spracht Zarathustra*. It was at Foucault's suggestion that Barraqué used the Nietzsche. The two men then developed a great enthusiasm for the Austrian novelist Herman Broch's *Der Tod des Vergil* (1945), which had just appeared in French translation.[12] It describes how Virgil is tempted, as he lies dying in Brindisi, to destroy the *Aeneid*. The densely written poetic novel, which was not destined to find a wide audience, is a long meditation on the impossibility of total knowledge and the vanity of all human activity. Passages from the novel became the raw material for Barraqué's most extensive piece: *Le Temps restitué*. Barraqué began work on it in 1957, but did not compete it until 1968.

In an interview given to an Italian journalist in 1967, Foucault describes Barraqué as 'one of the most brilliant and least recognised of the present generation'.[13] He was not alone in believing Barraqué to be brilliant. Writing on Western music after Webern in the January 1960 issue of *Esprit*, the music critic André Hodeir described *Séquence* as 'the major acquisition of twentieth-century music' and *Etude* as 'very strange and very captivating'. Barraqué did not live up to his early reputation. *Le Temps restitué* proved to be his last major work, and he completed only seven compositions in his entire career, which was disrupted by a turbulent personal life, over-indulgence in alcohol and a serious car accident in 1964. His works are not widely performed and, being very demanding of musicians and listeners alike, have never become part of the standard concert repertoire.

Little is known about the relationship between the two men. Their correspondence has never been published in full, and Barraqué's published writings are highly technical essays on musical theory. In an unpublished letter cited in Defert's 'Chronology', Foucault describes Barraqué as 'adorable but as ugly as a louse . . . when it comes to bad lads, his knowledge borders on the encyclopaedic'. From the little than can be gleaned from the available evidence, the relationship appears to have been mutually destructive, fuelled by alcohol and tinged with sado-masochism.

Foucault had taken piano lessons as a boy in Poitiers, but had abandoned the instrument. Music continued to be important to him, even though he found its beauty 'enigmatic', and he developed a good enough ear to distinguish between different recordings of the same piece. He particularly enjoyed Bach and Mozart, but also had a liking for contemporary music, even though he admitted to finding it difficult because it tends to make each of its elements into a 'singular event'. He regarded it as a musical equivalent to the modernism of Cézanne, Manet and the Russian formalists. It was, he believed, an antidote to 'pre-packaged culture' because it upset the 'lazy habits' of cultural consumerism. He never did understand how his colleagues and students could show such enthusiasm for Husserl and Heidegger and, at the same time, be so obsessed with obscure rock groups.[14] The encounter with the music of Barraqué and Boulez was part of Foucault's introduction to modernist culture. On 5 January 1953 he saw the first production of Beckett's *En Attendant Godot* at the Théâtre Babylone in Paris. Many years later, he would still remember it as a breathtaking production.[15] Beckett's novels also made a great impact on him, and he would frequently return to them. He was also reading Bataille and the essays published by the novelist Maurice Blanchot in the *Nouvelle Revue Française*, and they supplied an introduction to a modernist literature that rejected psychological realism in favour of an austere impersonality.

An even more decisive encounter came in the summer of 1953. Foucault was on holiday in Italy with Pinguet. They indulged in the usual sightseeing, but Foucault carried the same book with him wherever they went, and even read it while sunbathing on the beach at Cittavecchia. It was a French–German bilingual edition of Nietzsche's *Untimely Meditations*.[16] This was not something he would have studied at ENS. Nietzsche was not highly regarded as a philosopher in France at this time, and was usually seen as a literary figure. His reputation was also tainted by the association with anti-Semitism and even Nazism. It was Foucault's generation that turned him into one of the most important names in contemporary French thought. Indeed, one passage in *Untimely Meditations* seems almost to supply the programme for Foucault's later career. Observing that the history of everything that gives colour to life has still to be written, Nietzsche asks the rhetorical question: 'where would you find a history of love, of avarice, of envy, of conscience, of tradition, or of cruelty? Even a comparative history or at least of punishment is so far lacking completely.'[17]

The teaching in Lille was scarcely demanding and covered the same topics as the lectures Foucault was giving at ENS. He was a popular and respected figure. His trips to Lille usually allowed enough free time for lunch or a least a drink in the *brasseries* of the rue de la Liberté or the rue Nationale, where he would meet students and young teachers. It was in these circumstances that he encountered Jacques Bellefroid, a future novelist but at this time a *lycéen* who was being taught by Jean-Paul Aron. The conversations in the brasseries of Lille were lively and wide-ranging, moving rapidly from philosophy to art, cinema and politics and back again. Bellefroid was very struck by Foucault's almost precious diction. He made a great effort to keep his voice low and to avoid the higher registers he strayed into when he laughed. He spoke 'like a still', distilling his language word by word to produce 'a subtle alcohol with a powerful bouquet'.[18] Foucault was also a good listener and enjoyed this kind of informal exchange. He liked the company of young people and, although he never wanted to be a teacher in a *lycée*, he would probably have been a good one.

The positions in Lille and at ENS were both part-time and temporary, and Foucault's future was by no means certain. He had by now decided that his career did not lie in clinical psychiatry but he was still teaching psychology at a relatively low level. The relationship with Barraqué was tempestuous and potentially dangerous for both men. Foucault still appeared to have no particular ambition to write anything of his own. His introduction to Binswanger had been a commission, and so had *Maladie mentale*. So too was his next publication. In 1952 he was commissioned to contribute a study of 'Psychology from 1850 to 1950' for a revised version of a history of philosophy which had reached its fourth edition in 1886.[19] Not published until 1957, the study was little more than a competent survey of trends within psychology from John Stuart Mill onwards, and duplicated the lectures Foucault was giving in Lille and Paris. According to Bellefroid, he complained that he had been 'talked into' writing it by Aron and was not particularly enthusiastic about it. As so often in his subsequent career, Foucault now changed direction completely and, as a result of an almost chance encounter, suddenly left France to lead a nomadic existence in northern Europe.

Three

In October 1954 Foucault received a letter from someone he knew only by reputation. Georges Dumézil was Professor of Indo-European Civilization at the Collège de France but as a young man he had taught at the University of Uppsala. He regularly visited Sweden for part of the spring and summer, staying in a small flat lent him by the university. His friends there had recently told him that the Department of Romance Studies was looking for a French assistant and had asked him if he knew of a suitable candidate. The post in Uppsala was effectively in his gift, but no one came to mind immediately. Dumézil was now in his late fifties, had spent a lot of time abroad and had few contacts with the younger generation. By chance, he had mentioned the vacancy to his friend Raoul Curiel, an archaeologist and orientalist who had just returned from a dig in Afghanistan. Curiel had been introduced to Foucault by a mutual acquaintance and described him as the most intelligent *normalien* he had met for a long time. Dumézil made further enquiries and wrote to Foucault to tell him that the post was free and to ask him if he might be interested. The successful candidate would also be the director of the Maison de France cultural centre attached to the university. The post was prestigious, since Uppsala's university is the oldest in Sweden. Its attractions, he went on, included the Carolina Rediva library, which he described as one of the best in Europe.[1]

Next autumn, Foucault took up the post in Sweden. Although paid by the University, he was on secondment from his posts in

Lille and at ENS and was technically answerable to the Quai d'Orsay's department of cultural relations. In retrospective interviews, he explained that his decision to leave Paris was inspired by a search for greater freedom than he could enjoy in France. His personal life in France was, he felt, restricted, and Sweden had a reputation for liberalism. He had, he claimed, no ambition to write and had looked forward to travelling and living out of a suitcase for some years.[2] He might have added that his relationship with Barraqué was increasingly difficult and entering what proved to be its terminal phase.

He did not meet his patron before he left: Dumézil spent the summer and early autumn in Wales, and they did not meet until spring 1956. When they did meet, they ritually listed their respective academic titles, concluded that Dumézil had indeed taken his *bac* some years before Foucault, and toasted one another's health in schnapps. At which point, Dumézil, who was 28 years older than Foucault, proposed that they use the informal *tu* to one another. This was the beginning of a long friendship that meant a lot to both men and which lasted until Foucault's death. Foucault did address the older man as *tu*, but when he spoke of him to others, Dumézil was always *le professeur.*

If, as seems likely, Foucault was in search of greater sexual freedom, he must have been somewhat disappointed. Although it is Sweden's fourth city, Uppsala was small by comparison with Paris and the atmosphere proved to be more puritanical than Foucault might have hoped. The city was more famous for its thirteenth-century Gothic cathedral than for its night life. The university itself was small by comparison with Lille. It was also a strongly hierarchical institution in which observation of protocol and recognition of rank counted for a lot. At times, Foucault must have felt that he was living in a colder version of Poitiers.

Foucault's task in Uppsala was to promote French culture and the French language by organizing screenings of French films, putting on plays and giving public lectures. He was also required to give *ab initio* lessons in French to anyone interested. He proved to be good at his new job. He was a popular lecturer and drew an audience from both the university and the city. His chosen topics must, however, have shocked some of his listeners. One of the final lectures given in his first year was on 'The Conception of Love in French Literature: From Sade to Jean Genet'. Neither Sade nor Genet was standard fare at any Maison de France, and both were still surrounded by scandal. Most of Foucault's lectures were on much more conventional subjects such as Surrealism, René Char, modern poetry, Impressionist art and seventeenth-century tragedy. He also gave occasional talks at the Institut Français in Stockholm. Foucault welcomed and looked after visiting speakers, including Roland Barthes, Marguerite Duras, the novelist Claude Simon, and his old teacher Jean Hyppolite, who was on a lecture tour that took him to Uppsala, Stockholm, Oslo and Copenhagen in December 1955.

In cultural terms, the high point of Foucault's years in Sweden came in December 1957, when Albert Camus came to Stockholm to receive the Nobel Prize for Literature. The visit was marked by ceremonial dinners and receptions at the French embassy, with the Nobel presentation taking place on 10 December. Foucault was present in a minor official capacity, and was greatly impressed by Camus. On the following day, Camus's meeting and discussion with a group of students resulted in a notorious incident. A number of Algerian students were currently following courses in Sweden, and the insistent questions put to Camus about the political situation in Algeria, where a vicious war of independence had been in progress since November 1954, provoked him into making the notorious statement that, while he loved justice, he loved his mother even more, and therefore could not support the Algerian FLN's use of a terrorist violence that might hurt her. The improvised remark badly damaged Camus's reputation as a liberal humanist. Camus also had discussions with students in Uppsala, but precautions were taken to ensure that the questions related purely to literary matters and raised no political issues. Foucault was not involved in the increasingly vocal opposition to the Algerian war and could not dare to be, given his professional position. His friend Jean-François Miguel reports, however, that he did attend meetings organized by Algerian students, and did express – in private – broad sympathy with their goal of independence.

The French-Catalan Miguel was a biologist doing post-doctoral research at the university. He and Foucault quickly struck up a friendship, and began to dine together in Foucault's quarters in the Maison de France. They were soon joined by the physicist Jacques Papet-Lépine. The three settled into a routine of taking it in turns to cook in the evenings; Foucault specialized in pasta dishes and elaborated complex theories about the correct way to cook them. The French trio were regularly joined by the Italian language assistant and her English counterpart. The small group of friends also included Jean-Christophe Öberg, the son of a Paris-based diplomat and himself a future diplomat, and a young French woman known as Dani who had come – at Öberg's suggestion – to work in Uppsala as a secretary. She became Foucault's secretary at the Maison de France and also did some work for Miguel, whom she eventually married. The small French group soon acquired notoriety for their noisy – and frequently drunken – parties. More notoriety came Foucault's way when he acquired a Jaguar sports car. He had learned to drive in Poitiers, but many of his passengers report that he was a less than reassuring driver. The car, which was beige with black leather upholstery, was second-hand but still expensive, and was prone to mechanical problems. Yet Foucault was immensely proud of it, and even went through a phase of choosing his clothes to match its colour schema.

Foucault's retrospective comments on Sweden are not flattering. Most visitors recall the white nights of June when the sun does not

Michel Foucault
in Sweden in
the 60s.

set. Foucault, in contrast, always spoke of the 'Swedish night' and of
the gloom of days when the sun scarcely rose at all. While he appre-
ciated the silence and the reticence of Swedes, he also associated his
years in Sweden with the cold he disliked so much. Sweden also provided him with a grim vision of a future in which, in 50 or 100 years
time, everyone would be 'happy, rich and ascepticized'. Although
Foucault's experience of Sweden was probably not as grim as his
later comments suggest, he never displayed any great affection for
the country, which he regarded as too 'medicalized'. The main lesson
he drew from his experience was that a certain degree of freedom
could have as many repressive effects as a directly repressive society.[3]

If there was time for frivolity and drinking, there was even more time for work. It was during the years in Sweden that Foucault began to work every day in a library. It was in Uppsala that he discovered a vast collection of books on the history of medicine and related topics. At first, he was not entirely sure of what he was doing. This uncertainty would remain characteristic of the man: he did not work to preconceived plans and saw no point in beginning a book if he knew in advance how it would end.[4] Despite that, he had signed a contract with a publisher in Paris to write a history of psychiatry. There had also been talk of a 'history of death', but that came to nothing. Foucault abandoned the psychiatry project and simply ignored or forgot about his contract. Something new and different was taking shape. He was working on what was to become *Folie et déraison*, better known as *Histoire de la folie à l'âge classique*, which was originally the book's subtitle. The notes and files of quotations soon began to accumulate. Foucault now toyed with the idea of submitting his work in progress for a Swedish doctorate, and, at some point in 1957, showed his manuscript to Stirn Lindroth, a specialist in the history of science and the history of ideas and an important figure in the university hierarchy. Lindroth was by no means unsympathetic to Foucault and had invited him to dinner on a number of occasions. While he may have liked the man, he did not like the proposed thesis. It was, he thought, too prone to speculative generalizations and went against Uppsala's more empirical or even positivist traditions. Foucault's attempts to revise the manuscript did nothing to change his views. The rejection was probably the decisive factor in Foucault's sudden decision to leave Sweden. The published programme for the autumn term of 1958 at the Maison de France announced that Foucault would give a public lecture on 'Religious Experience in French Literature from Chateaubriand to Bernanos', but it was never given. Hurt pride or, less charitably, wounded arrogance does help to explain Foucault's departure from Uppsala, but it is also true to say that the nucleus of his social world was beginning to disintegrate: by the end of 1957 Dani, Miguel, Papet-Lépine and Öberg had all left. Foucault now began to think of submitting *Histoire de la folie* as a French doctoral thesis, and sent the bulky manuscript of over 1,000 sheets to Hyppolite, who was now ENS's director. Hyppolite was unsure what to make of it but thought it might have the makings of a thesis and advised Foucault to send it to Canguilhem.

The years in Sweden was a period of exile in only the most relative of senses. Foucault had little contact with his family, but he regularly went back to Paris and the encounters he had there were more important than anything that happened in Sweden. His first stay in Uppsala lasted only from October to Christmas. Back in Paris at the end of 1955, he was introduced by Robert Mauzi to Roland Barthes, with whom he was to enjoy a long friendship. Barthes was in an even more precarious position than Foucault. Having spent years in a tuberculosis sanatorium, he had been unable to take the *agrég* and was, at 40, still very much on the margins of the academic world, not least because he too was homosexual. He was supporting himself with freelance work and by acting as a literary adviser to a publishing company. He also had begun to write the mordant essays on the 'mythologies' of everyday life that were to be collected and published in volume form in 1957. It was only then that he began to gain more popularity, and only in 1960 that he would find a secure academic position at the Ecole Pratique des Hautes Etudes, where he would stay for the next 18 years.[5] Just as he was establishing a new friendship with Barthes, Foucault's relationship with Barraqué was coming to an end. There was an attempted reconciliation and Foucault spent at least part of the vacation with him before going into retreat at Le Piroir. When he returned to Sweden in March, he received the letter in which Barraqué broke with him. 'I no longer want to be either an actor or a spectator in this degradation.'[6] Barraqué died in 1973, finally defeated by his liking for *un petit vin blanc*.

Foucault was in a curious position. He had broken the terms of his contract and was, apparently, facing unemployment. Dumézil came to his rescue. Under the terms of a Franco-Polish agreement signed in February 1958, a Centre for French Civilization was to open in Warsaw in the autumn. At the same time, a Polish Cultural Centre would be opened in Paris. Paul Rebeyrol, who ran the language-teaching section in the Quai d'Orsay's 'cultural relations', was looking for someone to direct the new centre, and Dumézil knew just the man. The old networks were being exploited once again: Dumézil and Rebeyrol had been at ENS together. Foucault moved to Warsaw. As the first director of the Centre he came under the aegis of the university authorities, but he inevitably also had dealings with the embassy. From 1958 to 1960 France's ambassador to Warsaw was Etienne Burin des Roziers, a man with close personal and political links with De Gaulle. For both De Gaulle and his ambassador, Warsaw was a strategic window on the east. In 1958 Poland was in very poor condition. The purchasing power of the average wage was the lowest of the whole of Europe. Foucault had, as he later put it in, moved from a social-democratic country that functioned well to a people's democracy that functioned badly.[7]

After the Warsaw uprising of August–September 1944, the city had been almost totally destroyed by the Germans as the Red Army watched passively from the far bank of the Vistula. When Foucault arrived, much of the city was still in ruins. The Hotel Bristol, in which he stayed at first, has now been resurrected as the five-star Royal Meridien Bristol, but in 1958 the Art Nouveau building was far from luxurious, while the frequent power cuts meant that Foucault sometimes had to prepare his classes and work on *Histoire de la folie* by candlelight. The new centre he was supposed to be running had no equipment. Before he could start teaching, Foucault had first to procure such basics as tables and chairs, and obtain books and newspapers for the hypothetical library. He did so with his usual energy and efficiency.

Burin des Roziers was impressed by the new arrival and the two men soon established a working relationship based upon mutual respect. Their political conversations confirmed Foucault in his view that De Gaulle was not, as many on the left believed, some kind of neo- or proto-fascist. Burin des Roziers's cultural attaché had been granted leave to complete the doctoral thesis he needed to finish before returning to Paris, and was now working in solitude in the Carpathians. Foucault became his unofficial replacement. He travelled widely throughout the country to give lectures and talks: Burin des Roziers was particularly impressed by the lecture he gave on Apollinaire in Gdansk. He even offered to make Foucault his official attaché. Foucault was happy to accept, but only on his own terms, and wanted to establish a country-wide network of cultural centres staffed not by junior diplomats, but by the Polish specialists he would recruit from French universities. Due to what the former ambassador euphemistically described as 'unexpected circumstances', the plan came to nothing.[8]

Although Poland was becoming increasingly repressive, the university campus where Foucault worked was still an island of freedom, and he was beginning to make contact with local writers and intellectuals. This inevitably attracted the attention of the secret police. So too did Foucault's quasi-diplomatic status and his homosexuality, which was no secret on the university campus. The classic honey trap was set up. Foucault began an ill-advised relationship with a young man who was working as an informer. He was from a supposedly 'bourgeois-nationalist' background, and agreeing to become an informer was the price he had paid for his university education. The trap was sprung and Foucault was called in by his ambassador. He was advised to leave Warsaw as soon as possible. What Foucault called 'the stubborn sun of Polish freedom' made a lasting impression on him and inoculated him against Soviet-style socialism for ever.[9] His old 'philosophy teacher' Louis Girard reports him as saying that the only thing wrong with

Poland was the socialism. Although Foucault did not keep up any of the contacts he had made in Warsaw, he retained some interest in the country and, almost 30 years after he left it, Poland became the focus of his political attention.

The unfortunate incident in Warsaw had surprisingly little impact on Foucault's career in cultural relations. Burin des Roziers stood by him and gave him excellent references. A visit to an obviously tolerant Rebeyrol at the Quai d'Orsay was all it took to find a new position in Hamburg. Foucault was now director of the Institut Français there and moved into the accommodation provided for him in Heidmar Strasse. His responsibilities were the same as they had been in Uppsala and Warsaw. Talks were given and lectures were arranged. There was a production of a play by Jean Cocteau. Cocteau thanked him in June in a personal letter which Foucault kept for the rest of his life.

Although Foucault's position as director was quite exalted, he did not shirk from more humble tasks. When the novelist Pierre Gascar got off the train in Hamburg, he was expecting to be met by a driver or some minor functionary. He was in fact met by a lugubrious-looking Foucault who was holding a handwritten sign reading 'Institut français' and wearing a very Germanic felt hat. Gascar had come to give a talk at the Institut, but his main memory of his visit was the guided tour of the Sankt Pauli red-light district given him by the director. Foucault took him to a strip club and to seedy bars where young men greeted him as 'Herr Doktor'. Alain Robbe-Grillet, Barthes and Jean Bruce, the current king of French detective fiction, were other beneficiaries of this bizarre version of 'cultural relations' when they came to Hamburg to promote French culture. More conventionally, Foucault also took them on guided tours of the city's art galleries, with which he had become very familiar.[10]

In theory, Foucault's appointment was for three years, but his career once more changed direction. Having heard from Canguilhem that there was a position vacant at the University of Clermont-Ferrand, he decided to return to academic life in France, and was now determined to submit *Histoire de la folie* as a doctoral thesis. He was not in the strongest of positions. He never held a full-time position in a French university. Although *Histoire de la folie* was nearing completion, Foucault had produced little during his nomadic years. His only publication from this period was the translation (with Daniel Rocher) of the neuropsychiatrist Viktor von Weizsaker's *Der Gestaltkreis*, which appeared in 1958. Other than that, his publication record was not good. Verdeaux's translation of *Traum und Existenz*, with its lengthy introduction by Foucault, had not done well, selling only 300–400 copies in three years. The rest of the print run had then been pulped. Foucault himself was now dissatisfied with *Maladie mentale*. As Roger Bastide put it in his report on Foucault's doctoral submission, his early works were respectable but 'minor'.[11] Foucault had yet to begin publishing articles in learned journals and was therefore largely unknown outside a very small circle. On the other hand, that limited circle included some important names. Canguilhem, Hyppolite, Dumézil and Althusser were powerful men, and their names opened doors. It was Canguilhem who had mentioned Foucault's name to Jules Vuillemin, who was now in charge of the philosophy department at Clermont-Ferrand.

Both Hyppolite and Canguilhem had already seen versions of Foucault's manuscript. While Hyppolite had some reservations, Canguilhem was convinced that it was a thesis and that there was no need to change anything. In the preface to the first edition of *Histoire de la folie*, dated 'Hamburg 5 February 1960', Foucault acknowledges the help of Canguilhem, who 'advised me when not everything was simple',[12] and it is sometimes said that Canguilhem was his supervisor. Canguilhem always denied this. As *Histoire de la folie* was not originally intended to be a thesis, its author had no supervisor in the usual sense of the word. Foucault had worked in isolation in Uppsala, Warsaw and Hamburg. Most of the work was done in the library in Uppsala, but Foucault's footnotes and references indicate that he had also carried out quite extensive research at the Bibliothèque Nationale and the Archives Nationales in Paris.

At this time a doctoral candidate had to submit two theses. The main thesis was usually on a standard academic subject, and the shorter complementary thesis on a topic of more personal interest. Foucault inverted the convention. *Histoire de la folie* was his principal thesis, and his complementary thesis was a commentary on and translation of Kant's 'Anthropology from a Pragmatic Point of View'.[13] It is a solid piece of academic work that concentrates on conventional issues of textual dating and so on. It cannot have required an enormous amount of work, since Foucault had lectured on the subject at ENS and was quite familiar with the material. It was *Histoire de la folie* that posed the problem. Before his appointment at Clermont-Ferrand could be finally ratified, Foucault had to find a publisher for it. This did not prove straightforward, especially since Foucault did not want a purely academic readership and therefore rejected Delay's offer to publish it in a collection he edited for Presses Universitaires de France. He submitted it to Gallimard, then as now France's leading publisher, but it was quickly rejected. A very disappointed Foucault began to look elsewhere, and eventually sent the manuscript to Plon, perhaps encouraged by the fact that they had published Claude Lévi-Strauss's *Anthropologie structurale*, which had also been rejected by Gallimard, in 1958. He also had a contact at Plon; Jacques Bellefroid, whom he had met while teaching in Lille, was a reader there. Foucault recalled that a long silence ensued. When he went to Plon's offices in the rue Garancière to reclaim his manuscript, he was told they would have to find it before they could give it to anyone. It was eventually found languishing in a drawer and was passed on to Philippe Ariès.[14]

Ariès was not an academic, but an information officer with an institute established to promote the production and consumption of tropical fruit. The institute, a precursor of the later 'development aid agencies', had as strange a history as its information officer. It was established under Vichy, or in other words at a time when no tropical fruit could find its way into France and when French consumers could not have afforded it in any case. Ariès therefore spent the occupation years establishing a filing system. He also had a second life, and described himself as a 'Sunday historian' in the sense in which one speaks of a Sunday painter. He had recently published a highly innovatory history of childhood and the family. He continued to pursue both his careers, writing on a wide variety of historical topics, and being elected president of the International Association of Agricultural Information Specialists in 1970 and 1971.

Ariès was also something of an eccentric. As a young man, he had been an active member of the right-wing Action française group and he remained a devout Catholic and monarchist. He went to mass regularly, but in later years he did so wearing earplugs so as not to have to listen to all the 'nonsense' that had emerged from the Second Vatican Council. Ariès had never heard of Michel Foucault and was not a philosopher, but he was dazzled by the manuscript. His superiors were rather less impressed and it took a great deal of persuasion on his part to have the manuscript accepted.[15] Ariès persevered, and in May 1961 the book appeared in his *Civilisations d'hier et d'aujourd'hui* series.[16]

By October 1960 Foucault was back in Paris and once again living in the rue Monge. His appointment at Clermont was ratified that month. Once more, he was appointed to teach psychology. That same month, Robert Mauzi introduced him to someone who would change his life. Daniel Defert had just entered the École Normale de Saint-Cloud. He was in his early twenties, good-looking and lively. He was also a political activist who helped to organize opposition to the war in Algeria, now in its final phase. Foucault had never met anyone quite like him. The two men almost immediately embarked upon a passionate relationship.

Before long, they had decided to spend the rest of their lives together.

In France, the defence or *soutenance* of a doctoral thesis is a public event, and the Sorbonne's Louis Liard lecture theatre was crowded on Saturday, 20 May. Daniel Defert was sitting next to Jean-Paul Aron, and both Althusser and Canguilhem had encouraged their students to attend. The jury was, for reasons of seniority, chaired by Henri Gouhier. The complementary thesis on Kant was examined by Hyppolite and Maurice de Gandillac, who specialized in Renaissance and medieval studies, and *Histoire de la folie* by Canguilhem and Daniel Lagache, now Professor of Pathological Psychology. The *soutenance* began with a discussion of the Kant thesis, as summarized by the doctoral candidate. Gouhier was quite impressed with the commentary, but suggested that the translation could do with some revision. Otherwise, it could be the basis for a full critical edition. Foucault did not follow up that suggestion. The translation was published by Vrin in 1964, but the 130-page thesis was reduced to a very short historical introduction. After a short break, discussion turned to *Histoire de la folie* and there were further objections from the jury. Lagache challenged certain of the assumptions about the history of medicine and psychiatry, while Gouhier thought that far too much attention was given to Artaud, Nietzsche and Nerval. Despite the objections, which were only to be expected in the agonistic context of a *soutenance*, Foucault performed well. At the end of the afternoon Gouhier announced that he had been awarded the degree of *doctorat ès lettres*, as well as a bronze medal awarded by the Centre National de Recherche Scientifique.

Although it won Foucault his doctorate, *Histoire de la folie* was a rather curious thesis. There was no abstract, and nothing resembling a real introduction or conclusion. Foucault completely ignored the academic convention of reviewing the existing literature on his subject, and very rarely referred to any secondary sources. His methodology was not described in any detail, though most readers would have recognized a broad similarity with the so-called history of mentalities school. Historians associated with that school concentrated, like Ariès, on the slow, almost imperceptible changes in the way in which attitudes to death change and evolve over time, or at how notions such as 'childhood' gradually emerge.

Foucault's topic might crudely be described as the history of the slow transition from the old notion of 'folly' to the modern concept of 'mental illness' and its medicalization. *Folie* is an ambiguous term, and one that is not easy to translate. It covers both the idea of 'madness' and the much older and much vaguer term 'folly', as praised by Erasmus and as experienced by both King Lear and his fool. It can, that is, connote both madness and the higher form of reason available to the holy fool or visionary. *Déraison* ('Unreason') may look like a neologism of Foucault's making, but is in fact a medieval term denoting lack of reason in thought, speech or behaviour.

In Foucault's earliest writings, 'mental illness' was described as an individual mode of being in and perceiving the world, and the analysis focused on the experience of an individual subject. It now comes to be seen as a product of reason's exclusion and expulsion of all that it regards as 'unreason'. As Foucault was to put it in his first press interview, 'Madness exists only within a society' because it is society and its institutions that generate it by defining the forms of unreason.[17] The reason of the classical age breaks off the dialogue with madness that had once been possible in the Middle Ages and the Renaissance, and reduces it to silence. Foucault's first book attempts to recapture the history or archaeology of that silence.

The book opens with a dramatic reference to the disappearance of leprosy from Europe at the end of the Middle Ages. As the lazar houses begin to empty and as the lepers disappear from the deserted areas on the edges of the towns, a new fear begins to haunt Europe. A strange vessel drifts slowly along the slow rivers and canals of the

Rhineland and Flanders: the *Narrenschiff* or Ship of Fools with its human cargo of madmen and fools. If the Middle Ages had been haunted by the fear of leprosy and of death from war or plague, the Renaissance comes to be haunted by something that is intrinsic in the human condition: madness and unreason. In the works of Shakespeare and Cervantes, folly mocks at reason, as it does in the paintings of Bosch, Breughel and Goya, but it is not yet defined in medical terms. Folly was silenced by the Great Confinement of the seventeenth century or the classical age. In 1656 a royal decree established the Hôpital Général in Paris, and defined its mission as the confinement of the poor, the indigent, the sick, vagrants, mendicants, libertines and syphilitics.

The confinement of this heterogeneous population was not simply a committal of the insane, but an assimilation of the 'mad' to all the other categories that offended the canon of a reason that was confident about its own rationality. At the same time, a practical version of reason confined all those who were deemed to have transgressed the norms of their group or society. 'Madness' is not, then, a single category: unreason can be defined in legal, medical, social or even theological terms. It is the very existence of institutions such as the Hôpital Général that makes possible the emergence of clearer and more recognizable concepts of madness. In the seventeenth century institutions worked with constructs such as frenzy, delirium, melancholia and even stupidity; within a century, mad-doctors like Pinel and Esquirol were referring to conditions such as hysteria, hypochondria and nervous illness. To that extent, the founding of institutions like the York Retreat, founded by Samuel Tuke in 1796, represent not so much a response to a pre-existing definition of madness as one of the forces that define and create it. As in Canguilhem's history of the sciences, it is not empirical discoveries that lead to progress but the reorganization of the concepts that determine how an object such as madness or unreason is perceived.

Perhaps the most significant shift in the history of classical French psychiatry occurred when Philippe Pinel struck off the chains and manacles of those incarcerated in the Bicêtre asylum in Paris in 1794. Yet this was not simply an unambiguous liberation. Freed from their chains and the silence to which they were confined, the insane were now subject to the authority of their doctors. In the new regime instituted by Pinel, they now had to speak and admit that they were mad: the admission that they were mad was now a precondition for their treatment. It is this regime that facilitates the birth of clinical psychiatry. Here, therapeutic practice overlaps with and borrows from the religious notion of confession, to which Foucault would devote so much of his work after 1975.

One of the underlying theses of *Histoire de la folie* is that reason and confinement never succeeded in silencing unreason. The book, like the institutions it describes, is haunted by voices that murmur and mutter in the quasi-silence around madness. They are the voices of poets like Nerval, of the Nietzsche who proclaimed himself to be both Christ and Dionysus, of the Sade who takes Enlightenment reason to its ultimate limits and perverts it into its antithesis, of the Artaud who described Van Gogh as 'society's suicide' and whose language and reason literally disintegrated on the stage of the Vieux Colombier theatre in 1947. Their visual equivalents are the final paintings of Van Gogh and the nightmare visions of Bosch, and of Goya's *Disparates* and *Caprichos*. In contemporary terms, the voices of this murmuring unreason are those of the literary avant-garde. They are the almost anonymous voices that refuse to be silenced in Beckett's prose writings. Similar voices sing in the music of Barraqué and they speak in the transgressive texts in which Georges Bataille attempts to describe the *expérience-limite* that threatens to destroy reason and subjectivity alike. The voices would always haunt Foucault.

Four

The appointment at Clermont-Ferrand inaugurated a much more settled period in Foucault's life. For the first time, he had a permanent, full-time position in a French university. He had embarked upon a relationship with Daniel Defert that was to be stable, supportive and long-lasting, if not exactly monogamous. His first major book had been published and he had his doctorate.

Foucault's father died in September 1959. Relations between father and son may not have been perfect, but Foucault was left sufficient money to purchase an apartment. His new home was on the top floor of a high-rise block in the rue du Docteur Finlay in the fifteenth *arrondissement* and had good views of the Seine. The area was being redeveloped, and this was one of the first high-rise developments in Paris. Many found the area soulless, but it was modern and that was all that mattered to Foucault. Like Paris, France as a whole was embarking on an overdue period of modernization, but some things stayed the same or became even worse. In July 1960 the Assemblée Nationale adopted an amendment proposed by one Paul Mirguet. It committed the government to fighting a number of 'social scourges', namely tuberculosis, alcoholism, prostitution and homosexuality. Penalties for 'indecency involving individuals of the same sex' were increased to twice those imposed upon heterosexuals.

Foucault's appointment at Clermont-Ferrand did not change his habits. He never resided in the capital of the Auvergne and spent as little time there as possible, making the six-hour journey to the south by rail and staying overnight in a hotel before returning to Paris. His courses on social psychology and child psychology were farmed out to assistants and he concentrated on general psychology, which was defined in such general terms that he could talk about virtually anything. None of his lectures of this period has ever been published, and probably exist only in the form of notes but, assuming that Foucault followed his usual practice, at least some of them must have been early versions of *Les Mots et les choses*, the book that would propel him into the limelight in the summer of 1966.

The philosophy department was small, but Foucault had convivial colleagues. Six years older than Foucault, Jules Vuillemin was a distinguished scholar who had written widely on Kant, Descartes and the philosophy of mathematics and algebra. The younger Michel Serres had had a more exotic career than most academics, having taken a *diplôme de marine* at the École Navale before going on to take his *agrégation* in philosophy and a degree in mathematics. The only real problem was Roger Garaudy, who was the nearest thing the PCF had to an official philosopher and an influential member of its Politburo. Garaudy had already been many things, and would become many more. Originally a devout Stalinist, he was now an admirer of Khrushchev and the proponent of a mediocre Marxist humanism that Foucault loathed. To make matters worse, Garaudy was one of Althusser's most bitter critics, and Foucault remained loyal to his old mentor. In the 1970s Garaudy was expelled from the PCF for 'factionalism' and subsequently converted to Christianity and then to Islam before finally turning to Holocaust denial and anti-Semitism. For the moment, he was Foucault's *bête noire*. The department had wanted Gilles Deleuze, who had recently published his important *Nietzsche et la philosophie*, to have the post, but he was never appointed. Rumour had it that Garaudy had been foisted on the department at the insistence of Georges Pompidou. The notion of an alliance between a Communist and a Gaullist is less improbable than it might sound: the two had been at ENS together. Foucault could be as vindictive and cruel as he could be generous, and he wasted no opportunity to persecute and humiliate Garaudy, preferably in public. Few had much sympathy for the Communist, who was eventually forced out, and no one challenged Foucault's treatment of him. Foucault did, on the other hand, cause a scandal when he appointed Defert to an assistantship in preference to a better-qualified woman candidate.

Foucault's real life was in Paris. Despite the Mirguet amendment, it was much easier to be a gay man in Paris than in a provincial city. He was now dining regularly with Barthes, often several times a week, sometimes with other friends, but more often alone. It was easy to expand his circle of friends and acquaintances, to meet the artist and writer Pierre Klossowski through Barthes, or to meet the actress Simone Signoret and her husband Yves Montand at a social gathering. Foucault was also beginning to emerge as something of a public figure. On 31 May, only ten days after his *soutenance*, he was interviewed by Nicole Brice for French radio's 'France-Culture' channel. On 22 July a brief interview with Jean-Paul Weber appeared on an inside page of *Le Monde*. Foucault was described as the author of a 'remarkable' introduction to Binswanger and as having recently been promoted to the 'status of a well known or even famous philosopher'. Although brief and not terribly revelatory, these interviews were significant, since *Le Monde* had long been one of the main interfaces between the academic-intellectual world and an informed but non-specialist public. Foucault was always reluctant to be confined in the purely academic domain. Typically, he had not followed up Henri Gouhier's suggestion that he should turn his thesis on Kant into a full critical edition, and he never contributed to classically academic journals such as the venerable *Revue de Métaphysique et de Morale*.

Despite his increased visibility, Foucault's *Histoire de la folie* was not particularly successful. It was only in 1964 that the original print run of 3,000 copies finally sold out. It was not widely reviewed, but most of the notices were favourable. More important, they were by people who mattered to Foucault: Barthes, Serres, Lacroix, the historians Robert Mandrou and Fernand Braudel, and, most important of all, Maurice Blanchot. When the first edition sold out, Plon refused to reprint it in its original form. A drastically abridged version did, however, appear in 1964. It sold very well and was reprinted several times. Publishing serious philosophical and historical works in a *livre de poche* format was still something of a novelty, and Foucault was both pleased and amused to be published in the sort of collection that was sold on railway station bookstalls.

The Bibliothèque Nationale in the rue Richelieu was now Foucault's real place of work and he was there almost every day, cheerfully greeting acquaintances as he came and went but never discussing his work in progress with them. With its cast-iron pillars and glass dome, the main reading room was an agreeable place to work, particularly on dark afternoons when the individual reading lights at the desks bathed it in a calm, soft light. Foucault normally worked in the 'hemicycle', a raised area divided from the reading room by the enquiries and book issue desks and normally reserved for those consulting rare or fragile material. Here, he would work for long hours, taking notes on the books delivered to him and carefully copying quotations into the type of exercise book normally used in schools. The quotations would then be copied in black or light blue ink on to separate sheets kept in folders and filed by topic and theme. The files and folders also contained handwritten drafts of future works and innumerable projects, many of them never realized. Foucault frequently worked at home too, sitting cross-legged on the floor and using a board balanced on his knees as a desk. His working methods would never change to any great degree. They gave him a physical familiarity with his chosen texts that no other method can give. As he once remarked to his friend Claude Mauriac, copying out quotations by hand was both a 'banal and strange exercise' and a 'painstaking and obsessional occupation', whereas photocopying destroyed the charm of the text 'which becomes almost lifeless when you no longer have the printed page before your eyes and in your hands'.[1]

Foucault now began to publish widely, rather as though the publication of his first major work had released an enormous energy. Between 1961 and 1966 he published a series of articles and reviews in literary journals. They deal with Hölderlin, Raymond Roussel, Flaubert, Roger Laporte, the novelists associated with the journal *Tel Quel*, Mallarmé and the strange work of Klossowski, in which erotic and quasi-mystical themes merge to produce a very disquieting effect. It had once seemed likely that Foucault would become a psychiatrist; the emergence of a literary Foucault now looked more than likely, but he never really emerged. The real interest of these articles is that they outline a personal aesthetics for which the real subject of writing is language itself and in which there is no primal or pre-linguistic source of meaning. In the writings of Klossowski or Mallarmé, it is often difficult to say 'who' is speaking precisely because it is *language* that is speaking. What is heard in their work is a literary equivalent to the voices that murmur in *Histoire de la folie*, and it speaks of the dissolution of subjectivity and of the death of the traditional notion of the author.[2]

A much more sustained version of the same thesis can be found in *Raymond Roussel*, the only book Foucault devoted to a literary topic. As he explains in an interview with its American translator Charles Ruas, the book was born of a chance encounter. In the course of a visit to Paris in the summer of 1957, Foucault wandered into 'that huge bookshop across the road from the Luxembourg gardens'. The shop in the rue Médicis was owned by the bookseller and publisher José Corti. Waiting for Corti to finish the conversation he was having with a friend, Foucault idly glanced through an old yellow-covered book. It was a first edition of Raymond Roussels's *La Vue*, a long poem describing a seaside view engraved on a penholder. When he finally had the opportunity, Foucault asked Corti who Roussel was. Corti looked at him with an expression that clearly implied that everyone should know who Roussel was. Embarrassed at his own ignorance, Foucault asked if he could buy the book and always recalled that it was expensive. Corti then advised him to read *Comment j'ai écrit certains de mes livres*, in which Roussel explains the rigorous principles that govern his apparently chaotic narratives. Foucault had discovered a new enthusiasm that bordered upon the obsessional but kept it to himself: 'he was my love for several summers . . . and no one knew it'.[3]

Roussel (1877–1933) enjoyed almost no success in his lifetime. He was wealthy enough and eccentric enough to finance the publication of his books, to stage his plays and to absorb the heavy losses that inevitably resulted. The Surrealists had taken some interest in his work, but by 1957 he had been almost totally forgotten by everyone but a few connoisseurs, and Foucault had no real cause to be embarrassed by his ignorance. Roussel's works are based upon complex puns and shifts of meaning that are then used to generate fantastic narratives which, ultimately, are about nothing but their own production. Readers of the fourth (1932) edition of *Impressions d'Afrique* were advised by a pasted slip to begin with the tenth chapter, which opens thus: 'On 15 March the previous year . . .'. Such readers find themselves plunged into the adventures of a shipwrecked band of travellers who are being held to ransom in some African kingdom. As they wait for the return of the envoy who will bring the ransom, they prepare for the gala performance with which the book opens. It gradually becomes apparent to the patient reader that the novel is based upon a complicated pun. For Foucault, *Impressions d'Afrique* is a labyrinth of words, but it is dominated by death. One of the examples of word play within the narrative involves a loom (which weaves life and words) standing on a locked box resembling a coffin. Death is at the centre of the labyrinthine narrative.

Raymond Roussel was the first of Foucault's books to be published by Gallimard, and it appeared in May 1963. He also published a second book that month, and the two are at once very different and surprisingly similar. *Naissance de la clinique* appeared in a collection edited for Presses Universitaires de France by Canguilhem and it deals with the emergence of modern medicine.[4] The Roussel book is the most mannered, even precious, text ever written by Foucault. *Naissance de la clinique* opens with an austerely beautiful sentence whose poetic *gravitas* is hard to capture in English: 'Il est question dans ce livre de l'espace, du langage et de la mort; il est question du regard' ('This book is about space, language and death; it is about the gaze'). It is also about the changes that occur when doctors cease to ask 'What is wrong with you?' and begin to ask 'Where does it hurt?' It is about the emergence of what Foucault describes as 'the medical gaze'. The old medicine, rather like clinical psychiatry, classified diseases into 'species' related to one another by similarities and analogies: catarrh was to the throat what dysentery was to the intestines. Treatment could begin only when the species had been identified. The new medicine records the chronological development of the disease, and looks at how it inscribes its progress in the physical symptoms displayed by the body. The new medical gaze looks at bodies and not at abstract species. And it can do because doctors have heeded the advice of Bichat, the great comparative anatomist: 'Open up a few corpses.' The gaze can now focus on the spatial organization of a body: death is now called upon to explain illness and, ultimately, life itself. As in the Roussel book, death lies at the heart of the labyrinth. It is death and the dead body that provide medical knowledge of life, defined by Bichat as the sum of forces that resist death.

As he emerged more and more into the public sphere, Foucault made influential friends, but he also made enemies, sometimes in unexpected places. On 4 March 1963 Jacques Derrida gave a public lecture on 'the cogito and the history of madness'.[5] Derrida had studied with Foucault at ENS, and he began by praising his 'master' before going on to challenge his interpretation of a passage from Descartes. The main accusation, which was based on a very close reading of Foucault's text, was much more damaging: Foucault's attempt to outline the archaeology of the silencing of madness was in fact a repetition of the act perpetrated against madness. Worse still, the book was an expression of a structuralist totalitarianism that reproduced the violence directed against madness in the classical age. Foucault was in the audience, but said nothing. As Derrida must have known, Foucault was a man who bore grudges, sometimes for a very long time, and when he did finally reply, he did so in violent terms.

In 1963 Foucault and Barthes were invited by Jean Piel to join the poet and critic Michel Deguy on the editorial committee of *Critique*, the journal founded by Bataille in 1946.[6] When Bataille died in 1962, the editorship passed to Piel, who was anxious to breathe new life into the journal. Impressed by the article Foucault had published in the journal in the issue of July 1962 on two eighteenth-century novels and by *Histoire de la folie*, Deguy had written to Piel to suggest that they must have him on the board, and was probably unaware that Piel had met him in 1946. Both Foucault and Barthes accepted the invitation. Published monthly, *Critique* has always described itself as a 'general review of French and foreign publications'. The 'publications' in question were almost always literary or philosophical, and were discussed in long and serious review articles. *Critique* was not a political journal. Unlike the much older *Nouvelle Revue Française*, it was not part of the *belle lettriste* tradition and was always close to the avant-garde movements of the day. Unlike its main rivals, it was not dominated by any one tendency. *Les Temps modernes*, founded in 1945, was a mouthpiece for the Sartre-Beauvoir clan and *Esprit* was inspired by a left-wing Catholicism. *Critique*'s allegiances were purely intellectual and literary.

The first major task facing the new editorial board was the preparation of the special 'Hommage à Georges Bataille', due to be published in the autumn of 1963. The board and Piel held regularly monthly meetings, either in a restaurant or at Piel's home in Neuilly. The restaurant had to be close to the journal's office, since Piel's limp meant that he could not walk far. The office from which he edited the journal was in the premises of Editions de Minuit in the rue Bernard-Palissy, and was so cramped that it would have been difficult to fit four men into it. Happily, it was not far to Saint-Germain des-Prés, which abounded in bars and restaurants.

The Bataille issue appeared in August–September 1963 with contributions from Barthes, Blanchot, Klossowski and others. Foucault's contribution was a 'preface to transgression'.[7] Bataille's work covers an immense range of subjects from cave paintings to Manet, but is governed by themes deriving from the sociology of Durkheim and anthropology of the gift sketched by Marcel Mauss. Society is determined by the experience of the 'sacred' that lies on its margins and places limits on individual behaviour. He often refers to this as *l'experiénce-limite*. The sacred manifests its presence in extreme emotions, useless activity such as play or non-procreative sexuality and in bodily exhalations, all of which society would like to expel. Its truest expression is the potlatch ceremony of Native American culture in which great wealth is destroyed and given away in a conspicuous display of waste. Bataille also wrote erotica, but it is highly disturbing, since his vision of sexuality is both violent and excremental. Sexuality is a way of encountering and transgressing the limits of human society, and its ultimate limit is death. Eroticism encounters the limits in orgasm, the 'little death' that momentarily extinguishes any sense of individuality.

For Foucault, Bataille's work, like that of Nietzsche, is a response to the death of God and the void it creates, and it signals the demise of all philosophies of subjectivity.

The main product of the long hours and days in the library was *Les Mots et les choses*, published in April 1966.[8] This was the book that finally established Foucault as one of France's major intellectuals. The year 1966 was one of the most extraordinary in the history of French publishing. It saw the publication of Lacan's *Ecrits*, Barthes's *Critique et vérité*, which is his most devasting attack on traditional 'literary criticism', and the delicate structuralist essays collected in Gérard Genette's *Figures*. The previous year had seen the publication of Althusser's *Pour Marx* and the collective *Lire 'Le Capital'*. These were the years of structuralism and of what has come to be known, at least outside France, as 'French theory'. Extraordinarily complex and difficult books suddenly became bestsellers, though many more copies were bought than were read. Lacan's slogan 'the unconscious is structured like a language' was on everyone's lips, and even the austere Canguilhem was briefly fashionable. Foucault genuinely thought he had written a book for at best a few specialists; the original print run of 3,000 copies sold out within a week, and in August, La Hune, a well known bookshop in Saint-Germain, reported that it was 'selling like hot cakes'. In the first fortnight of the month, *Les Mots et les choses* entered the non-fiction bestseller list of *L'Express*.[9]

Les Mots et les choses quickly came to be regarded as one of the 'Bibles' of structuralism, but that perception is somewhat mistaken. The structuralism of the mid-1960s derives mainly from the work of the Swiss linguist Ferdinand de Saussure who, in his posthumously published *Cours de linguistique générale*, describes natural languages as systems of signs that function only because the signs that make them up are different. A sign consists of a signifier and a signified, and the relationship between the two and the objects they designate is said to be arbitrary: there is no extra-linguistic reason why 'cat' should designate a feline quadruped. Popularized by Barthes and others, linguistic structuralism developed into a system of analysis that could, it was thought, be applied to virtually any area. Although Foucault often gave lectures on structuralism and privately described *Les Mots et les choses* as his 'book about signs', he used the terminology of structuralism sparingly. His own analyses use categories that are wider than 'sign' and focus upon 'discourse', somewhat loosely defined as a rule-governed body of statements. If Foucault aligned himself with structuralism, he did so because he regarded it as a variant on 'the philosophy of concepts.' In this context, a 'concept' can be roughly described as an analytic category that is derived not from experience, but from the intellectual work that Althusser called 'theory'. The philosophy of concepts was closely linked to a theoretical anti-humanism that contends that human actions are not determined by conscious or thinking individual subjects, but by impersonal agencies such as the unconscious, economic and political structures or Foucault's *episteme*.

Its subtitle describes *Les Mots et les choses* as 'an archaeology of the human sciences'. Foucault uses 'archaeology', which would soon be replaced by 'genealogy', to mean an investigation into that which makes certain forms of thought possible and even inescapable. The investigation is into the natural history, economics and grammar and linguistics of the 'classical age', which, as in *Histoire de la folie*, refers to the seventeenth and eighteenth centuries. Foucault's thesis is that the body of knowledge produced in any given period is organized around its 'unconscious', or a stratum of rules of which its thinkers are not consciously aware. Without really knowing it, the naturalists, economists and grammarians of the classical age used the same rules to produce the very diverse objects of which they spoke. Their work was, in other words, governed by what Foucault sometimes calls a 'historical a priori'. His usual term for this 'unconscious of knowledge' is *episteme*, which is the Greek for 'knowledge'.

Like *Histoire de la folie*, *Les Mots et les choses* deals primarily with the shift from the Renaissance to the classical age, and with the movement from that age to modernity. For the thinkers of the Renaissance, the world was governed by the *episteme* of 'similitude': the world was a book and obeyed a vast syntactic system based upon a system of similarities and correspondences. Aconite, for example, had an 'affinity' with the eyes because of the signature contained in its seeds: embedded in white, their dark globes are what the pupil is to the human eye. In this system, writing is 'the prose of the world' and the world can be read like a book. This is the world through which Don Quixote wanders as though he were on a quest for similitude in which everything is a sign from the many romances he has devoured. The reason why he is a comic – and tragic – figure is that he is moving through the world of the classical age but reading it in terms of 'similitude'.

The *episteme* of Foucault's classical age is organized around a system of *mathesis*, or a general mathematical science of order, a *taximonia*, or a more empirical system of classification, and genetic analysis. Its modes of thought are analysed in chapters dealing, respectively, with 'representing', 'thinking', 'speaking' and 'exchanging'. Although the text is at times very dense, it is very seductive in its erudition. Foucault also has the talent to make something as dull as the political economy of the eighteenth-century physiocrats look interesting. Readers who are seduced by Foucault into looking at the physiocrats themselves are almost inevitably dismayed by their aridity, but they do illustrate one important feature of the classical age. Their insistence that the land is the sole source of wealth demonstrates that the knowledge of their age had no notion of the idea of production that is so important in Smith, Ricardo and Marx. It is, however, the discussion of 'speaking' that best exemplifies Foucault's concerns.

For the classical age, language is no longer based upon similitude and exists, rather, in the form of signs and discourse. Its analysis therefore takes the form of the examination of figures, or types of discourse, and of figures, or types of relations between words and their representative content. It is assumed that language is a medium capable of representing all representations and that it is therefore a universal. There must be one possible language that can grasp the totality of the world, and that language must take the form of an encyclopaedia. The 'general grammar' of the classical age concerns itself not with what we now understand by grammar, but with the representative function of language as such. It attempts to arrive at a taxonomy of languages, just as Linnaean biology attempts to arrive at a taxonomy or rational classification of living species. Such theories of language are haunted by a dream equivalent to the dream of an encyclopaedia that can encompass and classify the whole of human knowledge. The classical age dreams of a perfectly transparent language in which there is no gap between words and things, in which things can be named without any fear of confusion. The same dream haunts political economy: the analysis of wealth can be represented by *tableaux*. The word is of course ambiguous, and can mean 'table' or 'picture'. Hence the importance of the opening analysis of Velázquez's *Las Meninas*, which is reproduced in the text: Foucault's virtuoso description of the canvas turns it into a representation of the classical act of rep-resentation and of the space it opens up.

The epistemology of the classical age can also be characterized in terms of its gaps: there are no life sciences and no philology, but merely taxonomies of species and words. Everything exists in the timeless, abstract space of a *tableau*. The origins of modernity lie in the rejection and critique of classical epistemology. With Ricardo and Marx, wealth is no longer a system of representation, but a form of value resulting from a productive process. With Cuvier, the structure of organs is to be understood in terms of their function, and not their position in a taxonomic system. The concept of life itself is no longer based upon a distinction between the organic and the inorganic; it becomes the element that founds all possible variations to be observed in living creatures. And as the dream of the perfectly transparent language fades, it becomes possible to study existing languages as natural objects, thanks to the philology of Jakob Grimm and Franz Bopp. Foucault's archaeology traces the origins of the modern human sciences of economics, linguistics and the life sciences. It also predicts their demise. The avant-garde literature examined by Foucault signals what is beginning to happen: language is turning against grammar and contesting the relationship between form and being. It is not a transparent medium for the communication of thought, but a material force with a life of its own. *Les Mots et les choses* ends with a description of a face drawn in the sand being erased by the rising tide. It is the face of 'man', an invention of recent origin and one whose end is nigh. Nietzsche pronounced God dead; Foucault announces the death of man. Like Nietzsche, he caused something of a scandal.

Foucault's main contribution to the philosophy of concepts is his *L'Archéologie du savoir*, which appeared in 1969.[10] The book is in effect a methodological supplement or appendix to *Les Mots et les choses* and provides a more abstract model of the earlier book's description of Foucault's 'discursive formations'. Psychiatry, for example, is a discursive formation born of the intersection of medical, legal and criminological discourses that produces the objects it claims to be treating as it interacts with non-discursive formations such as institutions and power structures. Although the text offers an alternative to Marxist theories of ideology that ultimately see everything as an expression of economic relations, it has to be said that it is by far the most arid of all Foucault's books and becomes almost painful to read as the concepts pile up and are constantly defined and redefined.

In September 1966 Foucault suddenly decided to take up a post as Professor of Philosophy at the University of Tunis. Tunisia was an attractive prospect. The former French protectorate had been

Michel Foucault in
Tunisia.

independent for just ten years. The university was young and many
of its dynamic staff were on secondment from France. The conditions of employment were good, and Foucault was being offered
twice the salary he would have received in France. Foucault was
already quite familiar with the country. Defert had opted to volun-
teer to work there on a cooperation and development scheme as an
alternative to national service in the forces, and Foucault regularly
visited him in the southern city of Sfax. He had already fantasized
about buying a house in Sidi Bou Said, which was conveniently
close to the capital. Defert is still rather puzzled by Foucault's decision to go to Tunis but suggests that it was his way of giving him
more space. It is puzzling in other ways too. *Les Mots et les choses*
had made Foucault a very prominent figure who might have done

more to capitalize on his reputation. Although he clearly enjoyed his new celebrity, he also found it disquieting. He complained about the reduction of serious work to media trivia, and the fact that the press talked as much about sales figures as the content of the book. The ambiguity of his new status is signalled by an interview. Foucault gave many interviews in 1966, almost all of them about *Les Mots et les choses*. In October he was asked by the journal *Arts et Loisirs* to comment on the recent death of André Breton.[11] He gave a competent and well-informed interview, but he was no specialist and knew little more about the magus of Surrealism than anyone else of a similar age and with the same cultural baggage. He was dangerously close to being cast in the role of The Intellectual who is assumed, or even required, to be able to pronounce on anyone and anything, and he was never entirely comfortable in that role.

Foucault taught on the philosophy degree course, lecturing mainly on Nietzsche, Descartes and psychology, but also gave public lectures at the university and, on Friday afternoons, at a cultural centre known as the Club Tahar Hadad. In a sense the public lectures were a reprise of the type of talk he had given in Uppsala, Warsaw and Hamburg, and they drew a similar audience of students from the university and figures from the Francophone elite. He was by now a fashionable figure, and lectures on anything to do with structuralism were guaranteed to draw crowds. As always, he was a very attractive speaker and was described by one witness as striding up and down his rostrum like a young naval officer pacing the bridge of his command. The witness in question was from *Esprit* and he added that Foucault's ship was a man-of-war.[12] Foucault was indeed fighting a war at one remove as he defended *Les Mots et les choses* from its many critics. The book that was selling so well was also very controversial. The image of the imminent death of man that ends it provoked outrage among traditional humanists, including those associated with *Esprit*, who claimed that it was an inhuman exercise in nihilism. Rather different criticisms came from the PCF and the left. Foucault was criticized for his characterization of Marxism as an ideology that was a fish in the sea of nineteenth-century thought, and as a fish that died outside that context. It was also claimed that Foucault's archaeology was totally ahistorical. It is true that it is not easy to see how the shift from one *episteme* to another occurs, but the coded implication of such criticisms was that Foucault was denying the very possibility of historical change and, therefore, of any progress towards socialism. Sartre, in particular, complained that Foucault had replaced the motion picture of history with a series of static lantern slides. Because they ignored history, Foucault and structuralism were the last ramparts of a bourgeoisie that was afraid of being swept away by the tide of history. Foucault's response was to describe Sartre as the last philosopher of the nineteenth century.[13]

Although he lived briefly in a hotel when he first arrived in Tunis, Foucault soon found what he wanted in Sidi Bou Said. Perched on a steep cliff and overlooking the sea, the village was spectacularly beautiful and enticingly exotic. It was, one regular visitor noted in his diary, a place where one could buy ice cream from the Italian, octopus from the Maltese, beans with cumin from the Jew, and chick peas with red-pepper sauce from the man from Sfax.[14] It was home to a bohemian expatriate community, and Foucault fitted in well. But it was something of an artificial paradise. With its white-washed walls and its blue doors studded with nails, the village was certainly beautiful, but it was not the timeless, unchanged place it appeared to be. Although it dated back to the time when Tunisia was an outpost of the sprawling Ottoman Empire and looked perfectly preserved, it had been lovingly restored in 1912 by Baron Rodolphe d'Erlanger, a painter and musicologist who inherited an enormous fortune made from banking. The house rented by Foucault was reputedly once part of the stables owned by the Beys who once ruled Tunisia on behalf of the Turks.

Michel Foucault in Tunisia.

Foucault kept the interior cool and dark and began to work early in the morning. It was a very comfortable home, but, as always, there was also a hint of ascetism about it. Foucault adopted the local custom of sleeping on a *natte* – the North African version of a futon

– that could be rolled up during the day. It was here that he worked on *L'Archéologie du savoir.*

It was in Tunisia that Foucault began the morning ritual of shaving his head. He joked to Pinguet that this meant he no longer had to worry about losing what little hair he had left.[15] When he was introduced to Foucault for the first time, Jean Daniel, who was the founding editor of *Le Nouvel Observateur*, sensed that he was caught up in a inner debate with himself and was torn between the powerful temptations of voluptuousness and an equally powerful wish to channel those temptations into a methodical ascesis and even a conceptual exercise.[16] It is true that this is a retrospective account written shortly after Foucault's death, but it does capture Foucault's state of mind during his years in Tunis. Pleasures were easily available. Cannabis, known locally as *kif*, was not difficult to find and it was of good quality. Young sexual partners were on hand. Foucault could swim in the sea almost every day, sunbathe and go for long walks along the beaches. Yet no one reports the excesses of earlier periods. The heavy drinking was a thing of the past, and for the rest of his life Foucault rarely drank at all. Pleasure was no longer a matter of either frivolity or potential self-destruction. It was becoming part of a disciplined aesthetics of existence.

Sidi Bou Said was an artificial paradise in more senses than one. The village was peaceful, but Tunis was not. The Arab–Israeli Six Day War of 1967 led to riots in the streets. Jewish-owned businesses were burned and looted. The ugly outbursts of anti-Semitism, which greatly shocked the pro-Israeli Foucault, were in part an expression of a more general unrest. The student union was unsuccessfully trying to achieve more autonomy and to make itself independent from President Habib Bourguiba's ruling Destour party, and trivial incidents regularly escalated into serious confrontation. One of those arrested for handing out anti-government leaflets in 1967 was Ahmad Othmani, a student in his early twenties who had attended some of Foucault's lectures. Foucault gradually began to sympathize with his students, and did what he could to help them. At one point he hid the Roneo machine they used to print their leaflets in his garden. In June 1968 matters became increasingly serious.

Othmani had now been released, had gone underground and was now playing cat and mouse with the police. Foucault took the incredible risk of giving him sanctuary in his house. In the summer of 1968 the cat won. Othmani was arrested and put on trial for plotting against the state, membership of a banned organization, spreading false rumours and insulting members of the government. Foucault and others attempted to ensure that he had a fair trial. Their efforts were in vain. Othmani was brought before a special court in August. The day before his trial began, he had been picked up the secret police, beaten and tortured, and left unconscious in an alley. Othmani was found guilty and sentenced to twelve years; his French-born wife was deported. The university went on strike. Some of the French lecturers protested, and others left the country in a gesture of disgust. Foucault stayed on – and was criticized for doing so in some quarters – to offer logistic and financial support. Back in France, Jean-Pierre Darmon, who had organized pleasant musical evenings in Sidi bou Said, set up a defence committee and brought Othmani's case to the notice of the French section of Amnesty International, which 'adopted' him as its first political prisoner.

In Tunis, the cat began to play cruel games with its mouse. Othmani was arrested and tortured, released and rearrested. Released on medical grounds in 1972, he was placed under house arrest, and then sent back to prison, where he spent long periods in solitary confinement and went on hunger strike. Written in jail, his first- hand account of his imprisonment and torture was smuggled out of Tunisia and published in *Les Temps Modernes* in April 1979. The resultant publicity and increased international pressure on the Tunisian government led to his release and pardon in August of that year. He is now a prominent member of Penal Reform International.

Foucault's behaviour and sympathies had not gone unnoticed. He began to realize that he was regularly being followed wherever he went. He finally committed an indiscretion reminiscent of the incident in Warsaw. A boy who had spent the night with him asked to be driven home in the morning, and gave Foucault directions. The directions led him into an ambush and he was severely beaten by a group of men in plain clothes. He soon realized that he was taking too many risks and could easily receive something worse than a beating. It was time to leave Tunisia, and his plans to buy a house in Sidi Bou Said had to be abandoned. Ironically, the Tunisian government now awards 'Michel Foucault Grants' to promote Franco-Tunisian exchanges.

Five

In Tunis, a bewildered Foucault followed events in France as best he could. The 'May 68 events' began with relatively trivial protests. The universities were overcrowded and student numbers continued to rise inexorably. Students complained about the remoteness of author-itarian teachers who still delivered their time-honoured *cours magis-traux*, about the old-fashioned definitions of academic subjects and about their living conditions. The storm broke, first at the University of Nanterre and then in the Latin Quarter in Paris, where the Sorbonne was occupied. For the first time since the Liberation barri-cades appeared on the streets of Paris. A general strike involving nine million workers then brought the whole of France to a halt in June.

Maurice Blanchot met Michel Foucault only on one occasion, when they exchanged a few words in the courtyard of the Sorbonne in May. In his account of this incident (written in 1986), he then adds 'but they told me he wasn't there'.[1] Foucault would have enjoyed this version of events. As he put it in one of the lighter sections of the *Archéologie*, 'I'm not over there where you're watch-ing out for me, but here where I'm watching you and laughing.'[2] At times he did seem to have the gift of protean ubiquity. The distinguished intellectual and respected public figure was also a political activist and even something of a street-fighting man. The years in Tunis had radicalized him.

By the end of the summer France was back at work, and in the autumn the universities were functioning again. There was, however, still a lot of turbulence in the faculties and the *lycées*. Tear gas was a familiar smell in the Latin Quarter, and vans and coaches of CRS riot police all too common a sight. May had spawned a host of radical political groups, most of them as critical of the PCF as of the parties of government. Recent events had completed what the Algerian war had begun: they had put an end to what Foucault called the long period in which 'PCF, correct struggle and just cause were synonymous'.[3] The very definition of politics was changing. Education, culture and even sexuality were now political issues in a way that they had never been. As Foucault put it, he did not suddenly become political: politics had come to him.[4]

France, and especially young French people, were being influenced by outside forces too. The Cultural Revolution in China was disastrously misinterpreted as a spontaneous revolt rather than a murderous series of manoeuvres designed to eradicate Mao's opponents physically, and many of those close to Foucault believed themselves to be France's Red Guards. An Anglo-American counter culture of drugs and rock and roll was also having a huge impact upon a country that had yet to generate a rock culture of its own. The convergence of the counter culture and ultra-left politics gave birth to some very exotic groups, and few were more exotic than Vive la Révolution, whose main slogan was an eloquent expression of the feelings of many young people: '"What do we want?" "Everything"'.[5]

The great slogan of May had been 'This is only a beginning'. One group in particular was firmly convinced that this was indeed the case. La Gauche Prolétarienne (GP) was founded in the autumn of 1968 and was one of the main proponents of a distinctly French 'Maoism' that drew upon the native tradition of revolt from 1789 to the Resistance. The GP's view was that May had been the harbinger of a civil war that would lead to either a new form of socialism or the return of fascism. Its task was to prepare for the coming war by joining the 'masses' and 'proletarianizing' its own members, who were mostly students or graduates. Some adopted an extreme solution to the proletarianization issue by abandoning the intellectual life, concealing their pasts, changing their mode of speech and their accents, and trying to 'establish' themselves as factory workers in the hope of becoming the revolution's new cadres. In most cases, the only result was a great deal of personal misery and considerable psychological damage.[6] Foucault never became a member of the GP, although Defert and many of their friends did. In the eyes of the GP he was a 'democrat' to be used or even exploited. And he was happy to play that role. This was not always easy. Some of those in the GP had, like its principal war lord 'Pierre Victor' (Benny Levy), studied with Althusser but had now turned their backs of his exquisite 'theory' and were in a profoundly anti-intellectual mood. The philosophy of concepts had had its day.

After May, a series of reforms was introduced. The various institutions in Paris were restructured into thirteen 'units of teaching and research' within a new Académie de Paris. Modular degrees were introduced and continuous assessment was offered as an alternative to the old examination system. The cornerstone of the reforms of Edgar Faure, Minister for Education, was the creation of a new institution built on land leased from the army in the Bois de Vincennes on the eastern fringe of Paris, which was almost as far away from the troubled Latin Quarter as it was possible to get while still remaining in the capital. The prefabricated buildings in the woods went up quickly and by late 1969 the Vincennes Experimental University Centre was open for business.

Recruitment of staff began in the summer of 1968, when Foucault was still in Tunisia. He was contacted by Hélène Cixous – now very well known as a feminist novelist and dramatist, but at the time best known for her academic work on James Joyce – who wanted to know if he would be interested in joining the steering committee. He declined the offer, but indicated his willingness to establish and run the new philosophy department.

'Indisciplinarity' was Vincennes's watchword and Foucault envis-
aged a very untraditional department of philosophy. He wanted its
teaching to cover two main areas: the political analysis of society
and the analysis of a certain number of scientific domains. The
team recruited by Foucault was brilliant and highly politicized.
Etienne Balibar and Jacques Rancière were young associates of
Althusser, and members of the ENS seminar that produced the
collective *Lire 'Le Capital'* in 1965. Alain Badiou was still close to
Althusser but increasingly known to be a Maoist. Michel Serres
had worked with Foucault at Clermont-Ferrand. René Schérer
was a Fourrier specialist, and soon to emerge as a significant figure
in the gay movement. Deleuze declined the invitation to teach at
Vincennes on health grounds, but did join the faculty two years later.

Vincennes opened in December, but initially attracted disap-
pointingly few students. The new university was modern and well
equipped. The corridors were carpeted and the lecture rooms were
fitted with televisions and recording equipment. Vincennes was
also very remote. It was a long walk through the woods and park-
land to and from the nearest Metro station, and the bus service
that had been laid on was unpredictable and inefficient. There was
always something mysterious about this university in the woods,
and strange rumours began to circulate about what was going on
there. It was whispered that courses on sex were being taught
there, and that they included 'practicals'. Foucault was indeed giving
lectures on 'sexuality and individuality', but they dealt with the
topics of 'heredity' and 'racial hygiene' and had no more 'practical'
content than his course on Nietzsche and genealogy.

That the student body did not understand 'experimental' in
quite the same way as Edgar Faure soon became apparent when a
very different experiment got under way at Vincennes. For many
of the staff and students, the civil war that had begun in May 1968
would continue with the destruction of the state institution of
the university, and Vincennes was home to a Committee for the

Abolition of the Wage System and the Destruction of the University. The wage system was never in any real danger, but the university was.

On 23 January 1969 further violent incidents occurred in the Latin Quarter, where the Sorbonne and the University Rectorate were occupied. Clashes continued for most of the evening. When news of these developments reached Vincennes, a hastily convened General Meeting immediately voted to occupy one of the buildings. The entrances and stairways were barricaded with whatever came to hand – including the new television sets. Two of those involved were Defert and Foucault, the latter neatly dressed in a black corduroy suit. The building was quickly surrounded by riot police, who gave the protesters a simple ultimatum: they could either leave freely or face the consequences of their actions. Many knew from experience what was likely to happen to anyone who 'left freely' and attempted to walk through a gauntlet of CRS armed with heavy clubs, and decided to stay on the grounds that there was at least some safety in numbers. The assault came early in the morning when volleys of gas grenades were fired through the windows. As the police moved in, those inside retreated up the stairways, blocking the way behind them with anything they could find and then joining those on the roof in hurling missiles at the advancing CRS. The outcome of the first battle of Vincennes was quite predictable, and before long more than 200 people were being herded into the main lecture theatre. Defert and Foucault, coughing and spluttering with the effects of the gas, were among the last to be rounded up. All were taken to the Beaujon police holding centre and kept there overnight before being released, without being charged with any offence in most cases.

Those involved in the Sorbonne occupation fared less well. Thirty-four students were excluded from the university for a year and it was rumoured that they risked being forced to do their military service early. This was an ominous threat, since it was widely believed that militants who were drafted into the army under such circumstances would have a hard and dangerous time of it. On 11 February Foucault and Sartre, who had never met before, addressed a packed solidarity meeting in the Mutualité hall. Foucault somewhat disingenuously argued that the students had done no real damage, and that everything that had happened had been an understandable response to police provocation.

Life at Vincennes now descended into chaos. Vandalism was commonplace, and justified on political grounds. Violently aggressive political graffiti covered the walls and books began to disappear from the library at a frightening rate. Drugs were on almost open sale. More depressing still for Foucault, the department he had founded with such optimism was at war with itself. A Trotskyist faction led by Henri Weber thought it had an opportunity to turn the university into a 'red base' and to transform an avant-garde institution into the weakest link in the capitalist system. Maoist hostility to members of the PCF – staff and students – was overt, violent and physical. PCF members attempting to attend lectures were spat upon and physically intimidated. Students in one of Jacques Rancière's classes voted for the permanent exclusion of all PCF members; they left of their own accord. Balibar was one of principal victims of the Maoist groups. He was a member of the PCF, and close to Althusser. For the Maoists of the GP, the PCF was the bulwark of the bourgeoisie, and Althusser its main ideological bulwark. Balibar was therefore a legitimate target. His lectures were picketed and his classes were regularly disrupted. He finally gave up the struggle, wrote to the Ministry of Education and requested a transfer back to the secondary sector, although he subsequently enjoyed a distinguished career as a professor of political philosophy at Nanterre. Foucault himself came under siege. He was forced to stop giving formal lectures, and to take part in endless 'debates' and meetings that led nowhere. At times, he found himself being denied access to his own classroom and passed desultory afternoons in conversation with sympathetic colleagues, or even

gave up and went to the cinema. In the Department of Psychoanalysis, Lacan's daughter Judith Miller decided that one way to
contribute to the destruction of the system was to give credits to
any student who enrolled on her course, irrespective of whether or
not they actually attended at all. A further blow came in January
1970, when the new Minister for Education announced that the
Vincennes philosophy degree could not be validated or ratified. In
an angry interview given to *Le Nouvel Observateur*, Foucault now
described Vincennes as a trap: they had been granted freedom,
and were now being blamed for having taken advantage of that
freedom.[7] Angry with the Ministry, Foucault was also frustrated
by Vincennes itself. While he was sympathetic to all the student
protests, he also wanted to work and expected others to work too.

Despite this flurry of activity and the chaos at Vincennes,
Foucault was serious about his academic career, which was now
taking on an international dimension. In March he was invited to
the United States for the first time and gave lectures in Buffalo and
Yale. In September he was invited to Japan, where his work was
beginning to attract attention even though little of it had been
translated. The visit also provided an opportunity to reply to
Derrrida's criticisms of *Histoire de la folie* in a special issue of the
journal *Paideia.* Foucault defended his reading of Descartes, but
also made telling criticisms of Derrida's deconstruction, described
as 'a well-determined little pedagogy'. Derrida's notorious insistence
that 'there is nothing outside the text' gave, he pointed out, 'limit-
less sovereignty' to the 'voice of the master'.[8]

Work was always Foucault's first priority, but his days in the
Bibliothèque Nationale were now frequently interrupted by his
attendance at almost constant demonstrations and meetings. His
growing political involvement also resulted in a change in his publishing strategy. There were fewer contributions to journals such as
Critique as Foucault turned to the press, regularly publishing minor
pieces on political issues and giving interviews to dailies like *Le*

Monde and news magazines such as *Le Nouvel Observateur,* to which he had easy access thanks to his friendship with Jean Daniel. Some friendships began to fade, and others were forged. Foucault's relations with Barthes cooled and they now saw each other very rarely. Barthes viewed the politics in which his old friend was becoming involved with extreme distaste. Demonstrations were, he believed, no more than an expression of hysteria. The friendship did not die completely and Foucault was largely responsible for Barthes' election to the Collège de France in 1976.

Foucault was also involved in a very different and traditional form of academic politics. The sudden death of Jean Hyppolite in the summer of 1968 meant that there was a vacant chair at the Collège de France and that a replacement had to be found. The Collège de France was founded in 1530 to provide a counterweight to the medieval Sorbonne and was once known as the college of the three languages (Hebrew, Latin and Greek). It has no student body and awards no degrees or diplomas. Anyone is free to attend the lectures given in the rambling building on the rue des Écoles. The professors, all elected by their peers, have only one obligation: to lecture and give seminars on their research. The election of professors follows a peculiar pattern. An initial round of voting approves the establishment of a chair, and a second round appoints a candidate to that chair. Rallying support is a complex political manoeuvre involving a lot of networking.

There were two other candidates in 1970. Foucault had briefly known Yvon Balaval at the University of Lille. The other candidate was Paul Ricoeur, who was desperate to escape from Nanterre where, in a notorious incident, he had had a dustbin pulled over his head and shoulders by a student protester. Foucault's main campaign manager was Vuillemin. Dumézil had now retired and, as an emeritus professor, did not have the right to vote but he did write to former colleagues to rally support for his friend. Foucault also had the tacit backing of an invisible college that included

The entrance to the Collège de France, Paris, with the statue of Claude Bernard. Foucault was elected to the College in 1970.

Althusser and Canguilhem, both powerful and influential men. He circulated a privately published booklet describing his published work and future plans.[9] It ignores his early work and makes his career begin with *Histoire de la folie*. The document outlines what he calls a history of the knowledge invested in complex systems of institutions, and describes that knowledge as existing between the established sciences and the phenomena of opinion. The Collège voted to establish a chair in the History of Systems of Thought, and then elected Foucault to it on 12 April.

On 2 December 1970 Foucault delivered his inaugural lecture. Beautifully constructed, it is perhaps his greatest piece of oratorical rhetoric. He began by saying that he wished simply to slip unnoticed into the speech (*discours*) he had to make and to hear a voice saying: 'I must go on, I cannot go on, I must go on . . . '. He ended by explaining why he had such difficulty in beginning his inaugural: he would have liked to have been invited to speak by a voice he had heard long ago in a classroom at the Lycée Henri-iv, the voice of a man who was no longer there to hear him. The man was of course Jean Hyppolite. Foucault's opening words were a paraphrase of the last lines of Beckett's *L'Innommable*, a text that meant a great deal both to him and to Hyppolite.[10]

At the beginning of the new year, the lectures and seminars began. Foucault lectured on Wednesday at 17.45 on 'the will to knowledge', which contrasted Aristotelean and Nietzschean theories of knowledge, and ran a seminar on the history of penal psychiatry at 17.30 on Monday. The lectures were immensely popular from the outset and, like Lacan's seminar, became part of the great spectacle of intellectual Paris. The lecture room in which he habitually spoke beneath a portrait of Bergson could not hold everyone who came. Those who could not find a place in the main lecture theatre listened to loudspeakers in an overflow room. Few of Foucault's audience took notes, and most used the cassette recorders that were still something of a novelty. Foucault had no power to restrict the numbers since his lectures were, by statutory definition, open to all. By 1976 he was so frustrated by this that he changed the time of his lecture to 9.30 in the morning, naively believing that not many students got up early enough to attend at such an hour.[11] He was wrong, and they did get up. As he spoke to his vast audience, Foucault experienced a strange isolation and loneliness. Discussion was impossible and even taking questions from the floor was difficult. The seminar provided a more attractive environment, and was much more conducive to the collective work that he always enjoyed so much.

Two months after his lecture, Foucault inaugurated something different in a very different place. A hunger strike was in progress in the Chapelle Saint-Bernard, a cavernous space beneath the Gare de Montparnasse. The strikers were demanding 'political prisoner' status for the imprisoned militants of the GP, which had been declared a proscribed organization in May 1970. On the night of its prescription, a huge protest meeting was held at the Mutualité hall and at its height Alain Geismar called on everyone present to take to the streets. Immediately after the meeting, he was arrested for inciting violence and later sentenced to two years in prison. Jean-Pierre Le Dantec and Michel Le Bris, who were the editors of the GP's paper *La Cause du People*, were also in prison. Sartre became the nominal editor of *La Cause du Peuple* and both he and Simone de Beauvoir deliberately and defiantly courted arrest by selling it on the streets. The violence was now escalating dangerously. The police station in the place du Panthéon was fire-bombed and police vehicles had come under attack. It was widely believed that the police were now out to kill. Gas grenades were being fired at head height as offensive weapons rather than being used for crowd control. The round of violent protest, violent repression and further violent protests seemed to be endless.

It was against this background that the hunger strikes began, and it was in this climate that Daniel Defert became a member of the proscribed GP. He worked mainly with the 'political prisoners' support group, which attempted to help the families of those in jail, but his concerns quickly broadened. Inspired by the 'people's court' that had been set up in the northern town of Lens to undertake an investigation into the deaths of sixteen miners in an underground methane explosion, he was beginning to think about establishing a similar investigation into the conditions in which prisoners – and not just the GP's political prisoners – were being held in France's jails. The eventual result was the formation of the Groupe d'Information sur les Prisons (GIP).[12]

Its foundation was announced when Michel Foucault read out a statement during a press conference in the Chapelle Saint-Bernard on 8 February 1971. The situation in French prisons was, he stated, intolerable: prisoners were being treated like dogs and the few rights they did have were being ignored or violated. There was an urgent need for information about life inside, and the GIP's first task was to gather that information in preparation for a long campaign. A questionnaire was handed out, to be filled in by or with the help of former prisoners. It was to be returned to 285 rue de Vaugirard. The founding statement was made in the names of Michel Foucault, Pierre-Vidal Naquet and Jean-Marie Domenach. Vidal-Naquet and Domenach had been contacted by Foucault at the suggestion of a radical lawyer of his acquaintance. Both names had great symbolic importance. The Catholic Domenach was the editor of *Esprit*, which had been one of the major platforms for opposition to the Algerian war. Pierre Vidal-Naquet, a historian and professor of classics, had been vocal in his condemnation of the army's systematic use of torture in Algeria. Neither man had any great philosophical sympathy for Foucault – Domenach and *Esprit* had been very critical of *Les Mots et les choses* – but they worked well together and forged friendships based upon their collective activity.

The GIP was informal in the extreme. There were no membership cards and no constitution, written or otherwise. While Foucault was regarded by most as its 'leader', he regarded himself as participating in a collective project in which all individuals were equal. He spent a lot of time addressing envelopes and stuffing them with leaflets, being well aware that no political organization can function unless such mundane tasks are carried out. Meetings were informal affairs, usually held in Foucault's apartment. The GIP's membership was very varied. Some support came from the Maoists of the GP. A few former prisoners became involved,

Poster for GIP, the Groupe d'Information sur les Prisons.

notably the loquacious Serge Livrozet, a one-time burglar who was keen to argue that theft was a spontaneous form of revolt or rebellion.[13] He and other old lags enlivened the meetings by swapping stories about the time they had served and the harsh conditions they had survived. *Esprit*'s loose network of readers' groups provided many of the activists. Individuals joined because they admired Foucault, or because they were friends of Defert's. Other associates of the GIP could scarcely even explain why they were involved. Danielle Rancière was studying for a doctorate under Foucault's supervision and found it only natural to join him in the street. Hélène Cixous recalls that it was only after the event that she asked herself why she had become involved with the GIP.

The GIP was not a pressure group demanding reforms and it did not attempt to speak on behalf of prisoners. 'Speaking on behalf of others' was regarded as shameful by Foucault,[14] and the group's self-defined task was to empower prison inmates to speak for themselves. Most of the GIP's activities were at first relatively low key and on a fairly small scale. Members joined the queues of wives and relatives waiting outside La Santé and Fresnes to be allowed in to visit inmates. Leaflets were handed out, questionnaires were distributed, and the militants found that they were gradually being accepted. Prisoners' wives did fill in the questionnaires, and there is some evidence that they were also smuggled into the prisons. The questionnaires and other scraps of information gathered in the queues outside the prison gates were used to produce a pamphlet entitled *Enquête en vingt prisons* in May 1971. A further two pamphlets were published the same year: *Enquête dans une prison-modèle: Fleury-Mérogis* and *Suicides de prison*. All have the same general title: *Intolérable*. It sums up the motives of Foucault and his associates: they were acting not in the name of some political programme, but quite literally reacting against what they perceived as the intolerable. In the long term, their work probably had little impact. At the time, its powerful effect was to reveal that the world of the prison was beyond or outside the law, and that the prisons were not filled with major criminals but with minor offenders who were at risk. It also had practical effects. It was at least partly because of their campaigning that it was announced in July 1971 that prison inmates could have radios in their cells and receive the daily press.

Working with the GIP required physical courage. No one risked what Othmani was going through in Tunisia, but the threat of violence was real. Deleuze became involved in demonstrations and protests in the streets, even though he had a respiratory condition which meant that exposure to tear gas was a serious threat to his already weak health. On one occasion, Hélène Cixous found herself regaining consciousness in a chemist's shop she had no recollection of entering. Nor did she have any memory of the truncheon blow to the head that had knocked her unconscious to the ground. Foucault himself was arrested on a number of occasions, but was inevitably released without facing major charges. The arrests were a form of intimidation, and not a preliminary to taking anyone to court.

The GIP was soon given a new impetus by events within the penal system. In February 1971 a nurse and a social worker were taken hostage by prisoners in Aix-en-Provence and died in the police assault on the prison. In July a warder was shot dead in St Paul's prison in Lyon. A nurse and a warder were taken hostage in Clairvaux prison and were killed when police stormed the building in September. The Ministry of the Interior's response was to suspend prisoners' traditional right to receive Christmas food parcels from their families. On 5 December Foucault and a group of GIP supporters gathered outside the Ministry of Justice, but even though a delegation of women was allowed inside the building their discussions with officials were fruitless. Three days later, the Minister did make a concession: food parcels could be sent to women and minors by their families. Other prisoners could be sent parcels through the Red Cross or Church agencies. The inmates of France's prisons had been given the same status as prisoners of war. Hunger strikes began immediately, and on 5 December prisoners at the Centrale Ney prison in Toul, which is near Nancy, refused to go back to their cells after exercise. Later in the month, a full-scale mutiny broke out. Prisoners staged rooftop protests and parts of the jail were ransacked and set on fire. Three squads of riot police put down the mutiny with great violence. Riots and mutinies now spread throughout the prison system.

As the situation became more and more dramatic, the GIP held protest meetings and published what information it could. The most damning criticisms came from inside the system when Dr Edith Rose, the psychiatrist at Toul, wrote an open letter that was widely quoted in the press.[15] It spoke of the systematic use of violence against inmates who committed the most minor breaches of discipline. The use of straitjackets and other physical restraints was commonplace. Suicide bids were alarmingly frequent. Prisoners were often refused the medical help they required, and she was not being allowed to do her job properly. Inevitably, Dr Rose was forced to leave the prison service. For Foucault, Edith Rose was the prototype of the 'specific intellectual': she was part of a system of power, but had denounced what happened within in very specific and concrete terms. Traditional or 'universal' intellectuals spoke in the name of abstract and universal principles; specific intellectuals spoke of what they had seen, and on the basis of their concrete knowledge of the institutions in which they worked.[16]

The GIP was effective and could mobilize small groups at short notice. On the other hand, it was very difficult for it to expand. Trade unions and the traditional parties of the left were neither able nor willing to support Foucault and his associates. The membership of the great union federations included organizations representing prison officers, and the unions were not going to denounce their own. Even within the GP, there were those who thought 'common criminals' insufficiently proletarian to bother with. The GIP's other problem was structural. The main problem facing it was that prison populations are by definition unstable. Unlike Livrozet, many former prisoners are, for understandable reasons, very reluctant to identify themselves as such.

Although the GIP took up a lot of Foucault's time and energy, he was also actively involved with other ad hoc campaigns. When the journalist Alain Jaubert was seriously assaulted in a police van after having offered to go to hospital with someone who had been injured in yet another investigation, Foucault and members of the GIP took to the streets again in May 1972. When an Arab teenager called Djellali Ben Ali, who was certainly no angel, was shot dead in a long-standing dispute with a neighbour in October that year,

Foucault with Jean-Paul Sartre on a demonstration at the Goutte d'Or, Paris, 1971.

Foucault was one of those behind the ad hoc committee set up to investigate the case. Its investigations also taught him a lot about the conditions in which immigrants lived in the slums of the Goutte d'or, an area in northern Paris that he never had occasion to visit until now. When Mohammed Diab mysteriously died of gunshot wounds while in police custody in December 1973, Foucault and his associates launched another investigation, in the course of which Foucault was arrested and spent part of the night in a police cell.

The campaigns to investigate cases like that of Diab were expanded, mainly by the GP, into broader issues and the question

Foucault with Genet on an anti-racism demonstration after the death of
Mohammed Diab in police custody, Paris, 1972.

of Palestine came to the fore. 'Palestine committees' began to attempt to operate and recruit in the immigrant areas. The ostensible goal was to promote and organize solidarity with the people of Palestine, but many saw them as a means to the rather different end of recruiting immigrant workers to the cause of the GP. While the motivation was in no doubt, and in its own terms, honest, such campaigns also revealed the Maoist left's underlying romanticism. For activists working with a basically populist worldview, the most exploited were by definition the most revolutionary. It followed that unskilled immigrant workers, who were mostly North African, should be recruited to the cause.

It was against this background that Foucault was introduced to Jean Genet by Catherine von Bülow, whom he had first met on a beach in Tunisia. Once a dancer with the Metropolitan Opera in New York, she was now working for Gallimard and had been given the unenviable task of acting as Genet's minder. Genet had a tendency to 'dive' or to disappear suddenly to a hotel where no one could find him. He would then disappear just as quickly from the hotel, leaving instructions that his few belongings should be sent to Gallimard. Genet was not active in the GIP but did have some involvement in the Palestine committees and took part in their demonstrations. His logic was irrefutable. In the United States, he worked with the Black Panthers. In Palestine, he worked with the people of the camps. In France, he was a poet, and that was all he was.

It was during the Jaubert campaign that Foucault first encountered Claude Mauriac. Tall, thin and bespectacled, Mauriac seemed the most improbable of allies. The son of the Catholic novelist Claude Mauriac, he was a journalist and a distinguished novelist in his own right. As a young man, he had been a personal secretary to De Gaulle. Unlikely as it must have seemed to both men, he and Foucault became close allies and friends, and Mauriac's diaries provide an almost day by day account of Foucault's activities during this most turbulent of periods.[17]

The GIP was a short-lived organization. In 1973 it was dissolved to make way for a Prisoners' Action Committee coordinated by Livrozet. It was a child of its time, and probably could not have come into being at any other. It relied for support on the disaffection of so many young people and was a product of a period that was as creative as it was turbulent. At the beginning of the twenty-first century, press reports about the appalling conditions in French prisons again began to emerge. They were confirmed by the head doctor at La Santé, a very specific intellectual who described in print a fearful regime of malnutrition, bullying, assault and rape.[18] Her book certainly generated moral outrage, but not the formation of a new GIP. No one took to the streets.

The early 1970s also saw the sudden emergence of feminism and gay liberation. Feminism was of little interest to Foucault and had little impact on him, although he did publicly support the right to abortion and contraception. He has often criticized for his masculinist stance and it is true that neither the book on madness nor that of prisons looks at gender or takes account of the fact that women and men tend to be committed to both prisons and psychiatric hospitals for very different reasons.

The foundation of the GIP coincided almost to the day with the foundation of the Front Homosexuel d'Action Révolutionnaire (FHAR), which was not so much an organization as an explosion of desire and sexuality. An initial statement published in Vive la Révolution's paper *Tout* set the tone: 'Yes, we've been buggered by Arabs; we're proud of it and we'll be buggered by Arabs again'.[19] FHAR's noisy presence took the form of riotous 'general meetings' on Thursday evenings at the École des Beaux Arts in the rue Bonaparte, when more time was devoted to more or less public sexual activity than to reasoned debate. FHAR had no real organization to speak of and still less did it have a structured leadership: it simply existed in the here and now. It did have an iconic figure in the shape of the startlingly beautiful Guy Hocquenghem, who was

24 and already had a complex past.[20] He had been a member of the PCF, but had been expelled when his sexual orientation became too obvious. He had attended Lycée Henri-IV, and was admitted to ENS in 1965, but never completed his course. As a young homosexual, he had found life there just as difficult as Foucault had found it two decades earlier. On 2 January 1972 *Le Nouvel Observateur* published an interview with Hocquenhem entitled 'La Révolution des homo-sexuels'. Its historic importance is that it was the first 'coming out' statement to appear in the mainstream press. Gay liberation had not been on the agenda in May 1968, when posters announcing the formation of a 'Pederastic Action Committee' had been torn down and ripped up in the courtyard of the Sorbonne. Towards the end of 1972 Hocquenhem published his manifesto-like *Le Désir homo-sexuel*, which celebrates homosexual marginality and promiscuity as forms of sexual modernity. Gay liberation was now firmly on the agenda. Foucault was not active in FHAR, though he had friends who were, and had serious doubts about the very notion of sexual liberation, as would become very apparent from the first volume of his history of sexuality. There was also the issue of age. Like their brothers and sisters in the US, many of those associated with FHAR and the new counter-culture in general 'trusted no one over 30', and Foucault was now over 40.

Six

On 6 April 1972 the body of sixteen-year-old Brigitte Dewevre was discovered on waste ground in the decaying mining town of Bruay-en-Artois, some 40 kilometres north of Lille. Suspicion fell on Pierre Leroy, a local lawyer and member of the Rotary Club, and he was arrested and jailed pending investigations. The dead girl was the daughter of a miner and had grown up in the shadow of the spoil heaps. For the Gauche Prolétarienne, this was the ideal scenario: an innocent daughter of the people had been murdered by a son of the corrupt local bourgeoisie. A placard was erected on the crime scene to say precisely that.

The GP had been campaigning on the issue of silicosis, but it now turned its full attention to the Dewevre case. The local edition of *La Cause du Peuple* published blood-curdling calls for vengeance, spoke of 'social cannibalism', and was quite prepared to justify demands for Leroy's castration or even his death because they expressed a spontaneous desire for class justice. Foucault himself was suspicious of the idea of 'people's justice', which he discussed at some length in an interview with Levy,[1] but seemed at the time to believe that Leroy was guilty (he wrote nothing on the case). In the event, Leroy had to be released for lack of evidence. The murderer of Brigitte Dewevre has never been found.

Although the violence in the Bruay case was verbal, the GP did have tendencies that could have led it down the same path as the Red Brigades in Italy. It did have a clandestine military armed wing led by Olivier Rolin ('Antoine') and had carried out acts of industrial sabotage.² In March 1972 a young Maoist called Pierre Overney was shot dead by a security guard outside the Renault plant in Boulogne-Billancourt as he tried to hand out leaflets. His funeral procession through Paris was followed by an estimated 200,000 people. The marchers included Foucault and, more surprisingly, the usually reclusive Althusser, who remarked to his old student that they were not just burying a man: this was the funeral of *gauchisme* itself. He was right, and a certain political adventure was coming to an end.³

Four days later, the GP's military wing took its revenge by kidnapping a social-relations officer from Renault. He was subsequently released unharmed. His kidnappers had carried guns, but they were not loaded. The terrorist option had been rejected. Significantly, there had been widespread revulsion after the Black September attack on the Munich Olympics, which left eleven Israeli athletes dead. Events in the town of Besançon in 1973 also helped to unsettle the convictions of groups like the GP. A strike at the Lip watch factory evolved into a full-scale occupation that put the plant under workers' control. The Lip workers produced and marketed their watches with great success. The conclusion was inescapable: there was no need for GP and its like. In October 1973 the group disbanded.

The first year of Foucault's seminar was devoted to the topic of penal psychiatry. The raw material for both that seminar and the lecture course of 1974–5 on 'abnormality' was culled mainly from the *Gazette des tribunaux* and *Annales d'hygiène publique et de medicine légale*, which regularly published lurid accounts of murderers, hermaphrodites, degenerates and other social 'monsters'.⁴ The tales of servant girls who suddenly and inexplicably murdered the children entrusted to their care were of interest because of the way they revealed the intersection between medical discourses about insanity and legal discourses about criminality.

One tale in particular proved to be of great interest. In 1835 a young peasant called Pierre Rivière had slaughtered his mother, brother and sister with a sickle and then fled his pursuers to live rough in the Normandy countryside. When he was finally arrested and brought to trial, Rivière caused a sensation. The supposedly illiterate peasant, who was seen by some as little more than a village idiot, submitted a long and eloquent memoir to the court to explain his actions. He had, he explained, killed his mother because of the way she had persecuted his father, and his siblings because they loved her. Throughout, he had acted on the orders given him by God and the angels. Rivière was found guilty of murder and sentenced to death. The sentence was reduced to life imprisonment on appeal. He was the beneficiary of a law passed in 1832: anyone deemed to be insane could not be convicted of a crime. They could, however, be incarcerated on psychiatric grounds, and it was in prison that Rivière committed suicide in 1840. At a trivial level, the case amused Foucault, who had been at school with a boy called Pierre Rivière. Its real fascination was the light on important changes in the concepts of criminality and insanity.

The seminar group worked on the Rivière text for two years. Numbers fluctuated somewhat, but about fifteen people were involved on a regular basis. The published accounts were incomplete, but hinted that Rivière's manuscript could be found in the archives in Caen. The historian Jean-Pierre Peter was dispatched to find it. By some miracle, it had survived the bombing raids of 1944, which had destroyed much of the town's archives, and was transferred to the Bibliothèque Nationale, where it could be photocopied. The text was published in 1973, together with short 'notes' by eight of the seminar's participants. The 'notes' discuss the legal context, relations between doctors and judges and the concept of 'attenuating circum-stances', but they do not interpret the text. It is left to speak for itself, and the only explanation provided for the triple murder is Rivière's own. The book was a popular success and was even adapted for the screen by René Allio in 1975.[5]

Foucault did not often have the opportunity to enjoy this type of collective work. He had tried to keep the seminar 'closed', but the Collège's administration ruled that it, like the lectures, had to be open to all. The tape recorders reappeared, and the seminar effectively became another lecture course. The only other seminar to result in a collective publication was that of 1974, which alternated between the legal use and function of 'psychiatric reports' and 'the origins of the modern hospital' or 'curing machine'. This time, Foucault circumvented the Collège's statutes by privatizing his seminar. A small working part met in private, either in his office at the Collège, at his home or even in a café. The eventual solution to the numbers problem was simplicity itself. Foucault cancelled his seminar at the end of 1980, and gave lectures that lasted for two hours rather than one.

The seminar of 1973–4 focused on the emergence of identifiable health policies in the eighteenth century and on the professionalization of medicine in the same period. The main themes identified were the new focus on childhood, the medicalization of the family, the growing importance of hygiene, and the use of medicine as an agency of social control. Attention was also given to the emergence of the hospital as a specifically medical space with its own architectural and planning systems, as typified by the renovation of the Hôtel-Dieu in Paris in the late 1780s. The publication of the group's work went almost unnoticed, and only Canguilhem reviewed it.[6] It was work like this that gave rise to Foucault's concept of 'bio-power'. Bio-power refers to all the strategies born of the realization that governments have to deal with a population of living beings whose needs have to be met by social technologies that create as well as meet their needs in the domains of health care, housing, town planning, social work, education and so on. Foucault often refers to it as the government of the living. The government of the

West coast, its benign climate and its relaxed atmosphere. California was also home to a thriving gay culture characterized by a sexual openness that was still almost unimaginable in Paris. Although Foucault had little time to explore it on this brief trip, he would become very familiar with the many and varied pleasures it could afford him. One of them was LSD. Foucault had never taken the drug before, although he had described its effects in print. In the mid-1970s LSD was not a dance-floor drug to be taken for frivolous reasons, but something to be used in an almost ritual way. There was an aura of danger about it, but there was also the belief that it could open the doors of perception, as Aldous Huxley, citing Blake, put it in his 1954 account of the effects of mescaline. Foucault first took acid together with two gay academics. The setting for the trip was Death Valley, and the soundtrack a tape of Stockhausen. Some months later he spoke to Claude Mauriac of 'an unforgettable evening on LSD, in carefully prepared doses, in the desert night, with delicious music, nice people and some chartreuse'. His experience confirmed his belief that LSD allowed the user to experience a form of 'unreason' or madness that was not constrained by the dichotomy between the normal and the pathological.[9]

One foreign trip was undertaken for very different reasons. At the beginning of September 1975 the Franco regime in Spain executed two members of the Basque separatist group Euz kadi ta Azkatasuna (ETA) for the murder of a Civil Guard. Eight other militants from the Frente Revolucionario Antifascista y Patriotica (FRAP), including two women, were awaiting execution. There was worldwide revulsion, not so much at the sentences themselves as at the mode of execution: death by garrotting. Foucault and Claude Mauriac were told the news by Catherine von Bülow, who insisted both that something had to be done and that they were the ones to do it. Foucault knew little about Spain or ETA, although he did recall Spanish refugees arriving in Poitiers and regarded Franco as 'the bloodiest of dictators'.[10] Neither he nor anyone else knew much about FRAP, which was the military wing of a somewhat ineffective Maoist group that had been heavily infiltrated by the police. Even so, he was convinced that something had to be done and was willing to be involved. The final outcome was the dispatch of Foucault and five others to Madrid, where they hoped to present a petition drafted by Foucault and to hold a press conference to denounce Franco's barbarism. The episode ended in farce as all six were arrested and put on the first plane back to Paris. Foucault felt that he could sense the physical presence of fascism and was reminded of his childhood in Poitiers: 'We saw once again that sight we had known during the German occupation: the silence of the crowd, watching and saying nothing.'[11]

On 27 September 1975 five of the Spanish militants were executed, Franco's only concession to the storm of international protest being that they were shot and not garrotted. Nine European countries recalled their ambassadors from Madrid. The French Government said nothing. Spontaneous protests brought demonstrators, including Foucault, Mauriac and Defert, on to the streets of Paris and the Champs-Elysées became a battleground as they clashed with the police trying to protect the Spanish embassy. At the weekend, tens of thousands marched from the place de la République to the Bastille in protest. To his astonishment, Mauriac, a former secretary to De Gaulle, found himself marching and clenching his fist in support of FRAP, a clandestine organization that advocated terrorism. Neither Mauriac nor Foucault had ever condoned terrorism in print, and they had not defended FRAP's actions in Madrid. Nor did they condone the terrorism of Germany's Rote Armee Fraktion (RFA), better known in Britain as the 'Baader-Meinhoff Gang', and in France as *la bande à Baader.* But when Klaus Croissant, one of the lawyers who had defended members of the group at their 1975 trial, was arrested in Paris in late 1977 and was due to be extradited to face charges of supporting a criminal organization, Foucault was one of the fifty or so 'celebrities' who signed a petition in his favour. Writing in *Le*

Nouvel Observateur, he spoke of Croissant's inalienable right to have a defence lawyer, but did not condone the actions of his clients.[12] Very violent protests took place in Paris. Foucault was once more involved and suffered a broken rib when he was caught up in a police charge. The Croissant affair led to some strained personal relations. Foucault refused to sign a petition being circulated by Guattari because it described West Germany as 'fascist', and could not endorse Genet's claim that everyone should be 'grateful' to the RFA for demonstrating that only violence could put an end to the brutality of men.[13] The disagreement with Guattari led to an estrangement from his old ally Deleuze, who had been a close friend, and to a cooling of relations with Genet.

The Madrid episode may now look almost ridiculous, and the assumption that a group of self-appointed French intellectuals had a right to intervene was not without its arrogance. Yet there is something significant about the text read out in Madrid. It uses the language of universal human rights and of justice:

> We have always fought for this justice in Europe. Even today, we must fight for it whenever it is threatened . . . we are demanding that the basic rights of justice must be respected by the men of Spain, just as they are respected by men elsewhere.[14]

Foucault had clearly come a long way from the Maoism of the GP and its talk of summary 'class justice'. Two years later, he was the principal organizer of a reception to honour Soviet dissidents at the Théâtre Recamier as a way of protesting against Leonid Brezhnev's state visit to Paris. He once more used the language of universal rights. Only a few years earlier, many of those present would have been denouncing the Soviet President for his 'revision-ism' rather than his atrocious record on human rights. Foucault's change of political vocabulary can be seen as part of a broader political sea change. During the months that followed the Madrid escapade, André Glucksman and Bernard-Henri Lévy were working on books that were to be the bestsellers of 1977. The 'new philosophers' were about to take the stage. For many, the years of Marxism were coming to a close.

Increasingly, Foucault now spoke in terms of the rights of the 'governed'. The term reflects the direction that the lecture courses and seminars were taking. They were beginning to expand on the theme of bio-power by looking at 'government' or 'governmentality', which were terms used by Foucault to describe all the techniques and procedures designed to direct human behaviour. In the seminar of 1979, for example, Foucault spoke of 'the government of children', the 'government of souls', the 'government of a house' and the 'government of the self'. The last notion was to evolve into that of an aesthetics of existence. The idea of the 'government of souls', for its part, was at the origin of Foucault's growing fascination with the ritual technologies of confession and penitence.

In publishing terms, Foucault had been relatively silent for some time now and much of his energy had gone into his micro-politics, but he had not ceased to work. Probably begun in 1972 and completed in the summer of 1974, *Surveiller et punir* was published in 1975. The book opens very dramatically with two juxtaposed images. The first is a contemporary account of the public torture and execution of Robert-François Damiens in 1757. He had been condemned to death for an unsuccessful attempt on the life of Louis xv. His sentence was hellish: after having the flesh torn from his breast, arms and thighs, his right hand, which had wielded the knife, was to be cut off. His limbs were to be torn off by four horses galloping in different directions. In the event, the horses were not up to the task and a human executioner had to sever his limbs before they could dismember him. The text then quotes from a set of rules drawn up for a Maison des Jeunes Détenus in 1838. The inmates began their nine-hour working day at five in the morning in summer and at six in the winter. Two hours were devoted to their education. Silence was the rule. *Surveiller et Punir* is the history of the transition from a regime of power that operated in public and with great violence to one that functions in the silence of institutions such as La Santé. Damiens was guilty of an assault on the physical body of a king who also had a symbolic and immortal body, as described by Ernst Kantorowicz in his great study of 'medieval political theology'.[15] The appalling violence inflicted upon Damiens was a visible expression of royal power. Visible suffering now disappears: by the end of this transitional period, convicts were no longer marched in chains to the ports from whence they would be deported, but were transported in closed vehicles with individual cells. Incarceration becomes the new norm. The change was not necessarily a liberalization on the part of power: the goal was to punish less, but punish better.

The shift of emphasis was not restricted to the penal system: La Santé looks very like Sainte-Anne. *Lycées* can look like barracks. In schools, in the army and in the factories of the early industrial period the bodies of children, soldiers and workers become subject to new forms of discipline and are governed by new forms of power relations that make them both docile and useful, and the laws that determine prison sentences are but one expression of those power relations. Although Foucault no longer uses the term itself, the new discipline might be said to be determined by a new *episteme* exemplified by the words 'surveillance and punishment'. The mechanism of surveillance is typified by the 'panopticon' described by the English utilitarian philosopher Jeremy Bentham. *The Panopticon* exists in two versions: the full text included in volume IV of Bentham's *Collected Works*, and the shorter French version commissioned by the Assemblée Nationale in 1791. In 1977 the latter was republished with an essay by Foucault on 'the eye of power' and an afterword by the historian Michelle Perrot.[16]

The noun derives from the Greek *panoptos* ('seen by all') and *panoptes* ('all-seeing') and originally referred to a combined tele-

The walls of La Santé, Paris

and Ste Anne, Paris: hospitals that resemble prisons that resemble hospitals.

scope and microscope. The panopticon described by Bentham is a circular building with a tower at its centre. The tower is pierced by broad windows overlooking the inner side of the ring, which is divided into individual cells with windows facing the tower. A supervisor can observe the occupant of each cell: a madman, a schoolboy, a prisoner or a worker. Their visibility is the trap in which they are caught. The ideal panopticon was never built, but it did provide a model for actual prisons from La Santé in Paris to Strangeways in Manchester. The model prison of Fleury-Mérogis, just outside Paris, came into use in 1969, but it reproduces the panoptic design of the Petite Roquette, which was opened in 1836.

Cellular confinement is one of the ways in which disciplinary power individualizes its subjects. Just as the sodomite who committed an act becomes a homosexual with a past, a history and a psychology as well as sexual proclivities, the criminal becomes more important than his or her acts, as a proliferation of discourses, and not least psychiatry, codify criminality and criminals. Psychiatric reports, social enquiries and the collation of personal histories all combine to generate the notion of the 'dangerous individual' from whom society must be protected. Hence the minute investigations that were undertaken into the life, past history and character of Pierre Rivière.

The publication of *Surveiller et punir* seemed, like the publication of *Histoire de la folie* in 1961, to inaugurate a period of great creativity. On 5 November 1976 the front page of *Le Monde* announced the coming publication of 'six volumes by Michel Foucault'. The first of them appeared in December. *La Volonté de savoir* was described as the introduction to a multi-volume 'history of sexuality.' The forthcoming volumes were described as dealing with, respectively, 'the flesh and the body', 'the children's crusade', 'woman, mother and hysteric, perverts', 'population and races'. Although all these topics are touched upon in Foucault's lectures and elsewhere, the promised books never appeared.

Foucault begins by demolishing the so-called repressive hypothesis, according to which the nineteenth century, and Victorian Britain in particular, had been characterized by a silence about sexuality. This was not just a historical issue; the many and varied sexual liberation groups of the day were still speaking of the need to combat 'sexual repression' in the name of desire. From now onwards, Foucault speaks increasingly of 'pleasures' and not of desire. In doing so, he distances himself from the so-called philosophy of desire that was associated primarily with Deleuze and Guattari. In their *Anti-Oedipe* of 1972, the philosopher and the psychoanalyst outline a philosophy that departs radically from the traditional view that desire is a reaction to and a longing for an object that is absent, and insist that desire is a mobile force that creates it objects.[17] Dense and sometimes infuriatingly opaque, the book is also very funny, particularly when it rages against classic psychoanalysis's 'familialism', or in other words its reduction of every problem to the eternal triangle of 'mum, pop and me'. *Anti-Oedipe*, with its vision of an eternally circulating and creative desire, was immensely influential, and had a particular impact on Hocquenhem's version of gay liberation. In distancing himself from the philosophy of desire, Foucault was also distancing himself from one of the dominant strands of gay politics.

The main source of comments on Britain is Steven Marcus's *The Other Victorians*, which looks at the pornography that flourished in a period of so-called puritanical repression.[18] The nineteenth century was, on the contrary, the beginning of a period typified by a proliferation of discourses that incited talk about sexuality. The ubiquity of the imperative to speak of sexuality is neatly illustrated by the juxtaposition of two quotations. The first is taken from a manual for confessors: the penitent is subject to an injunction to tell all, to reveal all details about sexual acts, thoughts and desires. The quotation is from Sade's *120 Journées de Sodome*. The story-tellers who entertain the debauched libertines when they shut themselves away in their castle are required to 'tell all' in an obscene parody of the act of confession. This version of 'telling all' is, for Foucault, prefigured by Diderot's *Les Bijoux indiscrets*.[19] Written in 1747–8, the *philosophe*'s cheerfully obscene novella tells the story of the ruler of an imaginary country who acquires a magic ring. When the stone in the ring is pointed at a woman, it has the power to make her speak the whole truth. But she will not speak with her mouth: her 'jewel' or vagina will speak on her behalf. For a certain discourse on sexuality that prevails in Enlightenment philosophy, the theology of confession and pornography, truth is spoken by the genitals. Confession and telling all both provide the basis for the incorporation of 'perversions' into a scientific discourse about sexuality. The *ancien régime* had spoken of the act of sodomy; the new discourse of sexuality, which may be medical, legal and / or psychiatric, produces the species known as 'the homosexual'. Individuals committed acts of sodomy, but the homosexual has a past, a way of life, a childhood and a history, perhaps even a mysterious physiology. Homosexuality itself is broken down into sub-species: inversion, pederasty, psychic hermaphroditism. The new discourse on sexuality is easily summarized: 'tell me what you desire, and I will tell you what you are'. A similar shift can be observed in criminology: acts such as theft or murder become so many expressions of a type of individuality, as the law, social workers and the police define 'the dangerous individual' who exists even before he or she has committed any offence. Homosexuals and dangerous individuals now have a genealogy. The text outlines a dichotomy between an *ars erotica* and a *scientia sexualis*, between an economy of pleasure and an orderly regime of knowledge. For the former, sexuality is an aspect of the art of extracting a truth from pleasure, with 'pleasure' defined as both a practice into which individuals are gradually initiated and the recording of an experience. A *scientia sexualis* is concerned not with pleasure, but with the acquisition of forms of power-knowledge. It is motivated by a 'will to knowledge' akin to Nietzsche's will to power.

Foucault.

In this perspective, power is not simply repressive: it generates discourses rather than silencing them. It can be defined as the multiplicity of relations of force immanent in the domain in which it is exercised. It introduces norms for behaviour, and categorizes some forms of behaviour –and some individuals – as 'abnormal'. Its effect is to produce a certain type of knowledge about sex rather than to repress it. Nineteenth-century discourse on childhood sexuality – often focused on the prohibition of masturbation – is, for example, defined by relations between the child, its mother and father, teachers and doctors. This, presumably, would have been the subject of the promised volume on 'the children's crusade'.

It is in this context that Foucault begins to outline what he would eventually call an aesthetics of existence. *La Volonté de savoir* argues against the emphasis of 'sex-desire' and begins to make the case for a new economy of 'bodies and pleasures'. In an interview published to promote the book, its author declared himself in favour of 'the decentralisation, the regionalisation of all pleasures'. He spoke to another interviewer of the emergence of a movement that was not demanding more sex or more truth about sex, but manufacturing other forms of pleasures, relations, bonds and loves. He wanted to see 'the end of the dreary desert of sexuality, the end of the monarchy of sex'. Pleasure had to be freed from the identity of the individual subject and from all constricting discourses. The end of the monarchy of sex was, he thought, signalled by the publication of *La Mort propagande* by the young novelist and photographer Hervé Guibert: 'with filthy material, he constructs bodies, mirages, castles, fusions, tenderness, races, intoxication; all the heavy coefficient of sex is volatilized . . . '. He saw another sign in a book by Schérer and Hocquenhem, which demonstrated that children have 'a pleasure regime for which the "sex" grid constitutes a veritable prison'.[20] Foucault was on treacherous ground here: the 'book' was a special issue of Guattari's journal *Recherche* and it was entitled *Coïre*. Described as a 'systematic album of childhood' and beautifully illustrated, it was in fact a graceful apologia for paedophilia or 'man–boy love'. Scandals over paedophilia still lay in the future, and sections of the libertarian left were quite prepared to try to justify it in the name of sexual liberation.

Foucault was no paedophile, but he certainly enjoyed the company of young men like the 22-year-old Hervé Guibert. Guibert was a young man in search of a 'master'. His ambition to be a film-maker had been frustrated, but he was a talented photographer and regularly wrote on that subject for *Le Monde*. In the early 1970s he approached Barthes in the hope that he would help him to break into publishing, but rejected his alleged sexual advances on the grounds that he was not attracted to older men. He found his master in Foucault and became a close friend. Friendship was an important part of the aesthetics of existence, and Foucault had begun to surround himself with a court of younger men, although the friendships involved were not necessarily sexual. His young courtiers were, like Guibert and the literary journalist Mathieu Lindon, both artistically talented and good-looking. Being Guibert's friend or master was a risky occupation since one of his specialities was the betrayal of those close to him. His writings were to be the source of the 'scandals' that broke after Foucault's death. His startling good looks and charm did not prevent the American novelist Edmund White from seeing him as 'Sade in jeans'.[21] In December 1991 Hervé Guibert committed suicide by over-dosing on the anti-AIDS drugs he was taking.

Guibert's novel appeared in 1977, but the bestsellers of the season were Bernard-Henri Lévy's *Le Barbarisme à visage humain* and Glucksmann's *Les Maîtres-penseurs*. These were the classic expressions of the so-called New Philosophy. The expression *nouveaux philosophes* was coined by Lévy to describe the authors he published in a collection he edited for Grasset. Not a few of them were, like the Glucksmann who had called for the destruction of the wage system and the university at Vincennes only a few years earlier, former Maoists. Greatly influenced by Solzhenitsyn, whose *Gulag Archipelago* had appeared in translation early in 1974, they now came to the conclusion that the Gulag was as quintessentially Communist as Auschwitz had been quintessentially Nazi. Both forms of totalitarianism were, ultimately, expressions of the 'cold monsters' of Enlightenment and Hegelian Reason. According to Glucksmann, the great confinement described by Foucault in *Histoire de la folie* and the disciplined carceral regime analysed in *Surveiller et punir* were major stages in the development of a totalitarian rationality. Foucault was not unsympathetic to Glucksman's interpretation of his work and reviewed *Les Maîtres penseurs* in favourable terms in *Le Nouvel Observateur* in May.[22] The book illustrated the fact that the Gulag did not arise, as Althusserians were still trying to argue, because of Stalin's failure to read Marx and Lenin correctly.

The fate of Soviet dissidents now became one of Foucault's major political concerns. On 17 December 1976 he appeared on *Apostrophes,* which was French television's flagship arts programme. He had been invited to discuss *La Volonté de savoir,* but never mentioned it and devoted his allotted time on air to discussing a recently published account of the case of Dr Mikhail Stern, a senior Soviet doctor who had been sent to a labour camp because he refused to listen to the KGB's suggestion that he should use his parental authority to dissuade his sons from emigrating to Israel. Foucault's gesture of solidarity was both generous and genuinely sincere, but it left many viewers frustrated.

On 1 April 1979 the first issue of a new monthly appeared on 2,000 news-stands across France. *Gai Pied* was the first gay magazine to go on open sale in the country. Its appearance marked a change of tactics on the part of gay activists. After the short-lived explosion of FHAR, gay militancy had been focused on small Groupes de Libération Homosexuels, which were organized on a regional basis. Their campaigns for the repeal of the Vichy legisla-

Michel Foucault at home, 1977.

tion and the Mirguet amendment had been unsuccessful, and, while a new and more visible gay culture was emerging, it was still subject to repression and hostility. In 1976 a small group attempted to lay a wreath in memory of the gay men who were deported to the German camps during the Occupation. It was trampled to the ground. *Libération* was regularly dragged before the courts for publishing 'contact' adverts from gay men and women. *Gai Pied* was designed to allow gays to establish a new presence by becoming a journal for gay information, contacts and visibility. The magazine sold well and went weekly in the autumn of 1982.

Foucault had not been involved in the GLH's campaigns, but he knew many of those who had been, including Jean Le Bitoux, who now became a member of *Gai Pied*'s first editorial team. Le Bitoux always maintained that it was Foucault who came up with the magazine's title during one of the friendly dinners they sometimes enjoyed. The title is a clever pun: its literal meaning is 'gay foot', but *prendre son pied* is a slang expression meaning to have sexual pleasure, or 'to have an orgasm'. Foucault himself would extend the pun by referring to its contributors and readers as *gais piétons* or 'gay pedestrians'. The content of the magazine varied from local and international news of interest to the gay community to broad cultural coverage, a crossword and a cookery column contributed by the writer Yves Navarre. It also ran articles by and interviews with important figures such as Sartre and Jean-Paul Aron, in accordance with the old tactic of defying the government to ban a magazine publishing their work. The government did not oblige.

The first issue ran an article by Michel Foucault, written at the request of Le Bitoux. The short 'Un plaisir si simple' is a bitter-sweet meditation on the theme of suicide. Foucault muses about 'slender boys with pale cheeks' who spend their lives entering the antechamber of death and finally leave it, slamming the door on the way out. He argues the case for the right to commit suicide, and then suggests that potential suicides should have access to something akin to the 'love hotels' he had seen in Japan. They would be places 'in which you could seek out with nameless partners a chance to die without any identity'. It would be 'such a simple pleasure'.[23] *Gai Pied* was not the most obvious place to publish this strangely dreamy piece, but Foucault was anxious to make the point that gay men (the magazine's target audience did not include lesbians) should not be defined by their sexuality alone.

A month later, Foucault expressed his solidarity with a very different tendency within the gay movement when he accepted an invitation to speak at Arcadie's annual conference together with Paul Veyne – since 1976 the professor of Roman history at the Collège de France – Jean-Paul Aron and the great Anglicist Robert Merle. Founded in 1954 by the former seminarian André Baudry, Arcadie was France's oldest gay or 'homophile' organization. Its stated goal was to promote the acceptance and tolerance of gays, and discretion was its watchword. Its magazine, also called *Arcadie*, was mailed to subscribers under plain covers. Arcadie organized talks, cultural events and dances at which anything more than the slightest physical contact was frowned upon. Despite the emergence of new and much noisier organizations which despised it for its timidity and conformism, Arcadie continued to operate, and still held its dances in the faded splendour in a former cinema in the rue du Château d'eau near the Gare de l'est (the building is currently Paris's main temple to salsa music and dance). Foucault's contribution was a French version of the introduction to the English translation of *Alexina*. It begins by asking a question that would run through much of his later work: 'Do we *truly* need a *true* sex?' This deceptively simple question is an implicit challenge to any philosophy of desire and, more generally, to all forms of identity politics. It subverts the very notion of 'coming out' and, by extension, any statement that begins 'Speaking as a . . . I', because such utterances mimic the form of the confessional: 'Tell me what you desire, and I will tell you what you are.'

That Foucault could address such different audiences in such a short space of time once more reveals his ability to appear where he was not expected to be. Without actually taking sides, he offered support to two very different strands within the gay movement, as though to remind the new generation of gay activists that they did have predecessors and were all too quick to dismiss the brave work that had been carried out in a very difficult climate. As so often, his support for Arcadie was accompanied by a modest but telling gesture. At the end of the Congress, Baudry quietly slipped him an envelope containing a fee of 2,000 francs. Foucault immediately handed it back, and said that a gay man did not have to be paid to speak to other gays. Baudry is on record as saying that he was the only speaker to have refused a fee in the entire history of his homophile organization.

Seven

In April 1978 Foucault reverted to his old role of cultural missionary and travelled to Japan under the auspices of the French Ministry of Culture. On this occasion, he was accompanied by Daniel Defert. Their visit lasted for three weeks and allowed them to at least sample Japanese culture and hospitality. There was a screening of Allio's adaptation of *Pierre Rivière* and public lectures on familiar themes in Tokyo, but there was also time for discussions with representatives from a group of radical lawyers, with members of the Social Democratic Party and with some of those involved in the spectacular protests designed to halt the construction of the new airport at Narita. There was also an opportunity to visit some of Tokyo's gay clubs: 'They are tiny, and can't hold more than five or six . . . a sort of small, faithful and slightly mobile community.'[1]

Foucault's preparations for the trip had included a rapid immersion in popular accounts of Zen Buddhism, and the high point of the visit was a few days' stay in a monastery in the old imperial capital of Kyoto. Foucault was primarily interested in the self-disciplinary techniques used in meditation. He did attempt to learn them from the monks, but found the yoga positions involved both difficult to achieve and maintain. He was also keen to study a religion that, unlike Christianity, did not depend upon rituals of confession and penitence, but which was directed towards the enlightenment of the self and the ultimate realization that the self itself is no more than an illusion.[2] This was, to be sure, a fairly banal comment on the complexities of Zen, but it was consonant with Foucault's ongoing explorations into ways of marrying the care of the self to the deliberate and disciplined use of various pleasures.

Throughout the 1970s Foucault had combined academic work with hectic political activity. Increasingly, he wrote for newspapers and magazines rather than specialist journals. He was coming to believe that philosophers should become journalists and now became directly involved with a journalistic project. On 28 September 1978 the Italian daily *Corriere della Sera* announced on its front page that it had a new and distinguished commentator, and promised a series of articles entitled 'Michel Foucault Investigates'. He now enjoyed considerable popularity in Italy, where a collection of interviews and short pieces had appeared in translation as *Microfisica del potere* in 1977.

Foucault had been approached by Alberto Cavallari, who ran the Paris desk of *Corriere*, and their discussions resulted in a proposal for a series of articles in which 'an analysis of thought will be linked to an analysis of what is happening', or a new diagnosis of the present.[3] The series itself never materialized, but Foucault did contribute seven articles to the *Corriere* in the autumn of 1978. They were on Iran and were not published in French during Foucault's lifetime, but a lengthy piece in *Le Nouvel Observateur* served to summarize his views for a French audience.[4]

Foucault was not a professional journalist and had no specialist knowledge of either Iranian politics and history or the Shi'ite Islam that was mobilizing opposition to the Shah. Before going to Iran, he attempted to remedy his ignorance by talking to lawyers and human rights activists who worked with Iranian exiles in Paris and by having discussions with exiled members of the opposition. Armed with the little knowledge he was able to gather, he then made two visits to Iran in September and October. Days before his arrival in Tehran, the army had opened fire on demonstrators on Black Friday (8 September), killing thousands. Iran was poised for revolution and the return of Khomeini. The protests went on, as unarmed demonstrators again and again confronted the army. Foucault was convinced that there was no precedent for what he saw in Tehran and the holy city of Qom: 'a groundswell, with no vanguard and no party'. Events in Iran were an expression of 'a political spirituality'.[5] He did not believe that any one party would take power and that what he had seen was a genuine expression of the general will of the people. He did not foresee that after March 1979 a Khomeini government would replace secular despotism with a fundamentalist theocracy.

The articles were controversial and resulted in bitter criticism and attacks on their author. The myth that he was an unconditional supporter of Khomeini persists. In fairness, it should be said that he was not the only one to misread the situation. There was a fairly widespread belief in far-left circles in Europe, which had yet to discover what Islamic fundamentalism really meant, that forces like the Mujahideen guerrillas would emerge to lead a people's revolution. It is also true that Foucault was very quick to criticize the new Iranian regime for its abuse of human rights,[6] but there were no more articles for *Corriere dell Sera* and no more experiments in intellectual *reportage.*

Shortly after Foucault's return to Paris, a new word entered the French and English languages as the 'boat people' began to flee Vietnam on the frail craft that were so often wrecked or attacked by pirates in the South China Sea. On 8 November 1978 television audiences around the world saw the shocking pictures of a battered freighter with thousands of refugees on board being prevented from docking in Malaysia by the navy. At midnight, Dr Bernard Kouchner received an urgent phone call from the former Maoists Jacques and Claudie Broyelle. Kouchner was a former member of the PCF who had become immersed in humanitarian issues as a result of his experiences in Biafra in 1968. He was also one of the founders of the Médicins sans Frontières medical relief agency. The message from the Broyelles was direct and to the point: something had to be done. Kouchner immediately thought of Foucault, whom he had long admired both because *Naissance de la clinique* had impressed him as a medical student and because he regarded its author as someone who had always defended civil society against the state and 'power'.

The usual round of activity began. A statement and an appeal for funds to charter a relief ship were published in *Le Monde* on 9 November. Signatories were sought to endorse the appeal, and eventually ran into the hundreds. Foucault was at first reluctant to add his signature because he was by no means confident that the appeal would be successful, but he became a useful member of the Un Bâteau pour le Vietnam campaign, which was launched in a television interview with Montand on 20 November. The politics of such appeals are never easy. All France's Trotskyist organizations refused to become involved, and Communists grumbled about human rights being used to promote anti-Communism and to undermine détente. The involvement of glamorous figures like Montand and Signoret inevitably resulted in criticisms. Kouchner was accused of self-promotion and malicious tongues whispered that his boat was for Saint-Germain-des-Prés rather than Vietnam. The object of the campaign was at times in danger of being eclipsed by the attendant publicity, particularly when a much-hyped press conference held at the Lutétia hotel on 20 June 1979 became the occasion for a staged reconciliation between Sartre and Raymond Aron, once close friends and allies who had been sniping at each other for more than three decades. The campaign was, in the end, a success. A ship was chartered and sailed in April 1979.[7]

In the summer of 1979 Foucault finally gave up his old habit of working in the Bibliothèque Nationale on an almost daily basis. He was weary of the crowds and the constant delays in the book-delivery service. At a dinner party, he was introduced to a Dominican priest. Hearing of his problems at the Bibliothèque Nationale,

The Bibliothèque du Saulchoir, Paris.

Michel Albaric offered Foucault an attractive alternative. He was the director of the Bibliothèque du Saulchoir attached to the Dominican convent in the rue de la Glacière and he assured Foucault that he would find a warm welcome there. Foucault took up the invitation. The Saulchoir provided a pleasant working environment. Set back from the street, the small library is housed in an agreeable modern building built around a sunken garden. Foucault always worked at the same table by the window. The atmosphere appealed to him, and he joked to Claude Mauriac that 'If I were not a total atheist, I would be a monk . . . a good monk.'[8] The library's comprehensive holdings concentrate on theology and philosophy and provided the raw materials for both the second and third volumes of Foucault's history of sexuality, which focus on 'the care of the self' and the 'use of pleasures', and for the lectures on subjectivity and truth and the hermeneutics of the subject he gave at the Collège de France in 1981 and 1982.

The year 1980 began ominously and ended even more ominously when Althusser murdered his wife during a psychotic episode in

November and was committed to a series of psychiatric hospitals for the rest of his life. Foucault visited him regularly, and had already had experience of hospital visiting. On 25 February Barthes was hit by a delivery van as he was crossing the street outside the Collège de France and was rushed, bleeding and unconscious, to the Salpêtrière hospital. The accident did not seem to be particularly serious, and Barthes was soon receiving a steady stream of visitors, including Foucault, to whom he would mutter 'quelle bêtise' ('how stupid'). A month later Barthes died at the age of 64. According to his doctors, the accident had exacerbated Barthes' long-standing respiratory problems, but many believed that he had simply lost all will to live after the death of his adored mother in 1977. For Foucault, his friend's death was 'a scandal'. He was at the height of his intellectual powers and should have had years of productivity ahead of him. It fell to Foucault to read his eulogy to the assembled professors of the Collège. He paid tribute to a friend, a great writer and a wonderful teacher: 'Destiny would have it that the stupid violence of things – the only reality he was capable of hating – should have put an end to all that on the very steps of the house into which I asked you to invite him.'[9] Foucault himself had experienced the stupid violence of things in almost identical circumstances. In July 1978 he had been struck by a car as he crossed the rue de Vaugirard. He was flung into the air and landed on the bonnet of the vehicle. Shards of glass were embedded in his face and head and he spent over a week in hospital. Five years later he told a Canadian interviewer that his immediate reaction was a fatalistic acceptance of imminent death, but that it soon gave way to a 'very, very intense pleasure'. It was a beautiful summer evening and the near-death experience became 'one of my best memories'.[10] The pleasure may have been intense, but Foucault spent the next year suffering from bad headaches and bouts of nausea.

Sartre died on 15 April 1980, just two months after Barthes. Four days later his body was taken to the Montparnasse Cemetery.

It is estimated that between 200,000 and 300,000 mourners followed the hearse through the streets of Paris. There were scenes of near-hysteria, especially when Simone de Beauvoir had to be physically restrained from flinging herself into the open grave. Foucault was at first reluctant to attend the funeral. He had no sympathy, either personal or philosophical, for Sartre and actively disliked Beauvoir. He owed nothing to Sartre. Defert finally persuaded him that he had to attend, if only to demonstrate some respect for the role that Sartre had played as the prototypical 'French intellectual' of the post-war period. In the event, he found the funeral strangely moving, but there was no reconciliation in death. As he chatted to Catherine von Bülow, Foucault spoke with bitterness of the 'intellectual terrorism' that had been exercised by Sartre when he was a student at ENS.[11]

Although the discovery of the Saulchoir had solved his problems with libraries, Foucault was increasingly disenchanted with France. He had effectively broken with Deleuze over the Croissant affair and his articles on Iran had both cost him friends and left him bruised. In May 1980 the appearance of a new journal added to his discomfort. *Le Débat* was the brainchild of Pierre Nora, who had been Foucault's main editor at Gallimard from 1966. The title was chosen precisely because there was, in Nora's view, no true debate in France, and the first issue promised 'open debate'. It did not appear to be open to Foucault, who was not invited to contribute and who had not been informed of the project by a man whom he had long regarded as a friend. Nora's own contribution to the launch issue was an article on the public role of the intellectual, and it claimed that intellectuals' critical function often served to mask their crass political irresponsibility.[12] As presidential elections were due to be held within a year, the accusation of 'irresponsibility' was probably a criticism of the apparent reluctance of 'intellectuals' to rally behind François Mitterrand, who was the socialist candidate, and a similar refrain was heard after his victory, when there was disparaging talk of 'the silence of the intellectuals'. Foucault took it as a personal and very negative comment on his own political activities. The outcome was a violent quarrel with Nora. Foucault even threatened to leave Gallimard, and to publish the remaining volumes of his history of sexuality elsewhere.

Foucault's interest in prisons had not diminished and he was now involved with a campaign to defend Roger Knobelpiess, an armed robber whose criminal career had begun with a minor theft. Since 1976 he had been held in one of the new high security units that had been created in the wake of the mutinies and riots of the early 1970s. Solitary confinement and video surveillance were part of the regime of these contemporary versions of the panopticon. While he was in prison, Knobelspiess wrote his *QHS: Quartier de Haute Sécurité*, which is part biography, part a denunciation of the prisons in which he had spent so much of his adult life. Foucault wrote a preface to it, and turned once more to the question of the 'dangerous individual'. Knobelspiess had always denied having committed his first theft. Because he would not admit his guilt, he could not accept his imprisonment and repeatedly went on hunger strike and mutilated himself, but was not granted leave to appeal his sentence. And because he resisted his imprisonment, he was by definition a dangerous prisoner and was confined in a high security unit. He denied having committed a crime, but *could* have done so. The case also illustrated that prisons existed outside the law: no court could send Roger Knobelspiess to a high security wing, but prison officers could. In November 1981 Knobelspiess did go back to court on appeal, and was eventually pardoned by President Mitterrand. Two years later he was arrested again for armed robbery and shooting at two police officers. Foucault was much mocked for his support of a recidivist, even by people who, at the height of the GIP's campaigns, would probably have seen him as some kind of popular hero.[13]

As his discontent with France grew, so did Foucault's fascination with America, and particularly New York and California. At times, he even contemplated leaving France to teach in the States, and would certainly have had no difficulty in finding a chair there. In 1979 he had been invited to give the prestigious Tanner Lectures on Human Values at Stanford, and a year later he delivered a series of 'Howinson Lectures' on truth and subjectivity at Berkeley. In November he gave the James Lecture at the Institute for the Humanities in New York.[14] Lecture courses such as these were major events that drew large audiences and conferred superstar status on the lecturer.

In both California and New York, Foucault explored more of the gay scene, frequenting the area around Christopher Street in New York and the Castro district in San Francisco. An extraordinary number and variety of pleasures were now on offer in the back-rooms of the clubs and the bath-houses, which Foucault described as laboratories for sexual experimentation. The experiments were becoming more and more exotic as practices such as 'rimming' (anal-oral sex) and the self-explanatory 'fist fucking' spread. Dress codes such as the positioning of a handkerchief or keys on a belt signalled the wearer's proclivities and availability. The propensities of the leathermen in their chaps and chains were on open display. The sex was often with anonymous partners in darkened rooms and seemed to promise a new and liberating loss of individuality. Foucault was convinced that such encounters and especially sado-masochistic games were part of a 'whole new art of sexual practice' that went far beyond penetration and ejaculation. The innovations and variations on offer in the dark enhanced sexual acts, and extend-ed pleasure to the whole body and the mind. Sado-masochism, for its part, was an eroticization of power, a strategic game in which the role of master and slave could be inverted, reversed and then re-established. It extended pleasure far beyond the traditional pleasure of drinking, fucking and eating, as Foucault put in an interview with *The Advocate*.[15] This was a culture fuelled by drugs such as poppers (amyl nitrate capsules), a range of amphetamines and LSD. For Foucault, good drugs were essential adjuvants to the use of pleasures, but they were not to be used indiscriminately. Pleasure was too serious a business to allow the use of heavy opiates that might blur the delights of disciplined self-control. Foucault had serious doubts about the 'Californian cult of the self' and any theories holding that there was an 'authentic' self to be liberated, but agreed with Nietzsche that '*One thing is needful* – to "give style" to one's character – a great and rare art'.[16]

In the last two years of lectures at the Collège de France and in the second and third volumes of his history of sexuality, Foucault was proposing something very different: the active creation and care of the self, and the use of pleasures. 'Use of pleasures' is a translation of the Greek *chresis aphrodision*, described by Foucault as meaning the way in which an individual conducts himself, both in sexual and social terms, the regime that governs his conduct, and the manner in which he gives sexual acts a meaning in his life.[17] Foucault's last works are based upon a profound immersion in Greek, Roman and early Christian texts on confessional techniques and what Greek philosophy called 'truth-telling'.[18] They are austere, even dry, explorations into the origins of the notion of the 'desiring subject' and have little of the flair of his earlier work. If, however, they are read together with the scattered writings on the use of pleasures published in the gay press and with the late interviews, they become an intriguing introduction to Foucault's 'aesthetics of existence' and its combination of an almost stoic sense of self-discipline and a measured hedonism.

The Saulchoir was not Foucault's only place of work in Paris. He was also frequenting the 'Bastille Archive' in the Bibliothèque de l'Arsenal, where he went back to an old project. Sixteen years earlier he had signed a contract for a book to be entitled *Les Embastillés* for Pierre Nora's 'Archives' collection. It was never written, but

Foucault.

Foucault had not forgotten about it. In 1980 the historian Arlette
Farge was surprised to receive a package in the post. It contained
photocopies of Foucault's handwritten transcripts of a collection of
lettres de cachet from the Arsenal. A covering letter from Foucault
asked for her opinion as to the advisability of these requests to the

king to have certain individuals to be incarcerated indefinitely in the Bastille because of their debauchery, prodigality or unacceptable relationships. For Foucault, the fascinating thing about the letters was that they were not, as popular perceptions of *lettres de cachet* would have it, an expression of arbitrary royal power, but of demands from the families of the profligate debauchees. An absolute monarchy had made power available to quite humble families, and those families were ready to use it. He was also fascinated by the sheer beauty of the texts, and by the contrast between the florid style of the exordia written by professional scribes and the informal and often ungrammatical style of the letters themselves. Would it, he wondered, be a good idea to publish them as they stood and without any commentary?

Farge was both flattered and puzzled. She knew Foucault slightly, and greatly admired his *Surveiller et punir*. He had approached her because he had read her *Le Vol d'aliments* (1974), which is cited in *Surveiller et punir*, and her *Vivre dans la rue à Paris au XVIIIe siècle* (1979), which drew on archive material from the Arsenal to paint a very vivid picture of street life in eighteenth-century Paris. After much hesitation, Farge finally wrote to Foucault. She agreed with him about the beauty of the texts, but suggested that, while the letters could help to recover popular memories, they did require an introduction and at least a minimal commentary. Foucault rang back to say that he accepted her argument and to ask if she would be willing to work with him on the project. The collection of letters became *Le Désordre des familles*.[19] Touchingly, a note described the book as having been written in collaboration with the secretary who typed up Foucault's transcripts of the original letters. She did not live to see its publication.

The election of François Mitterrand to the presidency in May 1981 and the Socialist Party's victory in the legislative elections in June at last put an end to the long period of rule by parties of the right. Former Maoists and other leftists now moved close to the government and in some cases were given political positions. As the unrepentantly leftist Hocquenghem put it, those who had once worn Mao jackets were joining the Rotary Club.[20] Foucault did not join anything and remained in intellectual opposition. He had been in the place de la Bastille when news of Mitterrand's victory was flashed on to the big video screens, and was pleased with the new government's decriminalization of homosexuality and abolition of the death penalty, but remained sceptical about both the President and his government. Two years later, the scepticism of Foucault and others became the focus for a polemic over the 'silence of the intellectuals', who were accused by a government spokesman of rejecting politics and refusing to consider the issue of power.[21] It seemed to have been forgotten that it was obvious that Foucault was neither silent nor indifferent to the question of power in late 1981.

On 13 December General Wojciech Jarulzelski declared a state of emergency and destroyed any hope that a free and democratic trade union would be allowed to develop in Poland. Ever since the strike waves of the summer of 1980, Poland had been a popular cause in France, where there was a lot of support for Lech Walesa and his Solidarność movement. In late 1981 that support swelled. Solidarność badges sold well, and Foucault wore his for months. A statement was drafted by Pierre Bourdieu and Foucault calling on the new Socialist government not to make the same mistakes as its predecessors. A Socialist government had refused to send arms to Republican Spain in 1936, and a Socialist government had ignored the repression in Hungary in 1956.[22] Montand read out the statement during a radio broadcast on the morning of 15 December. He was appearing at the Olympia music hall; that night a Solidarność banner was lowered from the flies as he took his final bow. The government talked of non-interference in internal Polish affairs, but did take some action. Prime Minister Pierre Mauroy cancelled a planned official visit to Warsaw. Relief aid was sent to Poland.

Aid convoys were also organized by Médecins du Monde, which dispatched truckloads of medical equipment and food to Warsaw. The last of the sixteen convoys left in the autumn. One of the minibuses was carrying printing equipment and books as well as medical supplies. There were five passengers: Michel Foucault, Simone Signoret, Bernard Kouchner and two other doctors from Médecins du Monde. The five were a cheerful band and sang as they made the long drive to Warsaw. Their repertoire included songs associated with Piaf and Montand and, to his companions' surprise, Foucault knew all the words. Unfortunately, he could not sing in tune. It was only when they were well on the way that he told his friends something that very few people knew: he had lived in Poland. With great glee, he also recounted how and why he had been obliged to leave Warsaw in a hurry.

Warsaw was grim. Signoret noticed that the queues outside the shops were even longer than those she had seen in occupied France, and described the hotel they stayed in as being full of 'bogus prostitutes and real spies'.[23] In practical terms, the group could do little. They were received by the Minister for Health, who thanked them for the medical supplies but was not pleased when Foucault refused to shake his hand. Enquiries about the health of Lech Walesa went unanswered. The five were not in Poland for long but they did make a pilgrimage to Auschwitz. They walked in silence through the camp and stood for a moment in the square where the roll call was taken. Kouchner was astonished how small it was. He had somehow imagined that the six million victims of the Holocaust had once stood there. Foucault never spoke of what he felt in that square.

In May 1982 a new lecture tour took Foucault back to New York and then to Toronto. In the Canadian city, the bath-houses and saunas had been closed on public health grounds. Foucault's reaction was given in an interview to *Gai Pied*: there could be no compromise, and gays had to be intransigent. The law and the police should have nothing to do with the sexual lives of individuals. On this, there could be no compromise.[24] The real threat did not, however, come from the police. On 3 July 1981 the *New York Times* had run an article under the title 'Rare cancer seen in 41 homosexuals'. The following year, issue 34 of *Gai Pied* covered the first wave of cases of Kaposi's Sarcoma and spoke of 'US Gay Cancer'. Within a year, 27 similar cases had been reported in France. Many, especially within the gay community, were sceptical about the news. The idea that a disease could attack a particular group defined by its sexual orientation seemed simply laughable, and Foucault himself scoffed at the idea of a 'gay cancer'. In October and November 1983 he was teaching at Berkeley, where he delivered a series of six lectures on *parrhesia* or 'truth-telling'. As always, there was also time for more relaxed conversations with students, often over coffee. One such conversation turned to the subject of AIDS and Foucault remarked with considerable bravado 'How can I be scared of AIDS when I could die in a car? . . . If sex with a boy gives me pleasure . . .'. In retrospect, such pronouncements sound reckless to the point of folly, but the sentiments that inspired them were widely shared at the time. *Gai Pied* had run an article entitled : 'So fucking is dangerous, is it? And what about crossing the road?'[25]

Shortly after his return to Paris, Foucault encountered Alan Sheridan, an old friend and the translator of several of his books. They had not met for some years, and Sheridan was shocked to find that his friend looked ten years older than he was and that he had lost so much weight. Foucault had no idea of what was wrong with him, and nor did the doctors he had consulted. Sheridan and Foucault did discuss the possibility of AIDS, but Foucault dismissed the idea.[26] He had always been fit and healthy and there are no records of his having suffered any major illnesses as an adult, but in the summer of 1982 he did begin to suffer from persistent sinusitis and to complain of feeling tired. That did not prevent him from enjoying a holiday in Andalucia in the spring of 1983, or from continuing to exercise with weights. His condition did, however, begin to take its toll. On 28 March 1984 he gave his last lecture at the Collège de France on 'the courage of truth'. He was too tired and weak to go on. Even so, he corrected the proofs of his forthcoming books and was still angry enough to sign petitions in protest at the eviction of squatters in Paris.

By December 1983 Foucault's condition forced him to have his lungs examined. Antibiotics gave some remission. He did not ask for any diagnosis, and was not given one. On 3 June 1984 he collapsed at home and was immediately hospitalized in a private clinic on the advice of his brother. Six days later he was transferred to the neurology ward at the Salpetrière hospital. Having been moved to the Intensive Care Unit on 10 June, he enjoyed a slight remission. Over the next two weeks, his condition did improve somewhat. He was still talking about buying a house near Poitiers, receiving visitors and grumbling when tests and scans prevented him from watching the tennis on television. He read the first reviews of his new books. To his joy, a letter from Deleuze signalled their reconciliation. The hopes of early June proved to be false, and Michel Foucault died on 25 June 1984.

As soon as the news that Foucault had been hospitalized, rumours about his condition began to spread. Now that he was dead, they became even wilder. In an effort to put an end to them, his doctors and family took the highly unusual step of releasing a press statement about the cause of death. Foucault had been suffering from septicaemia, which resulted in serious neurological complications that had spread to his brain.

It was announced that Foucault's funeral was to be strictly private, and the ceremonial removal of the coffin from the hospital was the only opportunity for many people to say a last farewell. On Friday, 29 June a crowd gathered in the courtyard outside the Salpetrière's mortuary. Friends from the different periods of Foucault's life mingled: comrades from the activist days with the

Gilles Deleuze
reading from *The
History of Sexuality*
as Foucault's coffin
is taken from
hospital and
placed in the
hearse.

GIP and in the Goutte d'Or, representatives from Gallimard and
Seuil, the director of the Bibliothèque Nationale. Georges Dumézil
tried to comfort his daughter, who was Foucault's godchild, and
Montand supported a Simone Signoret who was on the point of
collapse. Mauriac mourned together with his daughter Natalie,
who had dined with Foucault on 30 May and who had been
shocked by the state in which she had found him. Three red roses
had been placed on the coffin, together with a card that simply
read 'Mathieu, Hervé, Daniel'. Deleuze read out a passage from
the introduction to *L'Usage des plaisirs*.

The coffin was sealed and lifted into a hearse to begin the final
journey back to Vendeuvre-du-Poitou, where Foucault was buried
within sight of Le Piroir. The ceremony was something of a compro-

mise. Mme Foucault, who outlived her eldest child by two years, had wanted a religious service, but Defert demurred as politely as he could. Foucault was buried by Michel Albaric. Well aware of the delicacy of the situation, he had suggested a 'service of absolution' rather than a full Requiem Mass, and orchestrated a combination of prayers, silence and meditation. When the moment came, he dropped roses into the grave: 'May God keep you, Michel'.

The press release giving Foucault's cause of death failed to stop rumours spreading. Although it was published in *Le Monde* and elsewhere, the press attributed Foucault's death to a variety of causes over the next few days. Some papers (*L'Humanité*, *Le Point*, *Le Figaro*) did not report any specific cause of death, while *La Croix* spoke of a brain tumour. In England, *The Times* simply reported that Foucault had 'died suddenly', while *The Guardian* spoke of a 'rare brain infection'. The *New York Times* reported a 'neurological disorder' but also stated that 'the cause of his death was not immediately disclosed'. On 26 June *Libération* published a special 'Foucault' issue. It contained fulsome tributes and reminiscences by many who had known him. It also contained an unsigned note criticizing the rumour that he had died of AIDS: 'As though an exceptional intellectual seemed, because he was also homosexual – a very discreet one, it is true – an ideal target for the fashionable disease . . . As though Foucault had to die a shameful death'. It is difficult to imagine a more tasteless comment. The newspaper Foucault had helped to found in 1973 was now confirming the rumour it claimed to be dispelling and insinuating, under the cover of anonymity that there was something 'shameful' about his death and even his homosexuality. As an angry Hocquenghem was to remark later, the paper had acted in bad faith to hint at the real cause of death without saying what it was doing. Hocquenghem also died from AIDS in 1988, but regarded his illness as a private matter: there was no categorical imperative to 'come out' about suffering from AIDS.[27]

Libération had, unwittingly or otherwise, initiated a nasty controversy. Even uglier rumours were circulating. Foucault had, it was being said, known that he had AIDS and had knowingly and deliberately passed on the virus to his sexual partners. Such rumours are of course part of the folklore that has grown up around AIDS. An equally pernicious version of events was published by Foucault's old friend Jean-Paul Aron. Aron was diagnosed as HIV-positive in January 1986. Almost a year later, he published a lengthy account of his condition in *Le Nouvel Observateur.*[28] 'Mon SIDA' is both brave and moving, and was the first account of AIDS to be published by a 'prominent figure'. Although Aron had the grace to admit that his spiteful comments about *Les Mots et les choses* had been motivated by jealousy, he also claimed that Foucault had always been ashamed of his homosexuality and had remained silent about the nature of his illness because he was ashamed of that too. This story continues to circulate. Writing in *L'Humanité* on 2 March 1999, the columnist Régine Desforges wrote that Foucault had died without ever having 'admitted' the nature of his illness, and contrasted his cowardice with the bravery of Aron and later victims such as Hocquenhem and Hervé Guibert, who had the 'courage to say what was killing them'.

Precisely how, where and when a given individual contracts the Human Immunodeficiency Virus is impossible to determine unless that individual has had very few sexual experiences and partners. It is almost as impossible to determine precisely what Foucault knew about his condition in his last years. There was in fact little that could be known. By July 1984, 180 cases of AIDS had been reported in France, and there had been 74 deaths. Five new cases were being reported every week. Ninety per cent of cases affected gay men, and ninety per cent of those men lived in Paris. Their doctors had little idea of what was happening to them. A possible viral cause had been identified and isolated in May 1983, but it was not until the following year that a link was established between HIV and

AIDS. An HIV test was devised towards the end of 1984, but was not available for general use until mid-1985. Foucault could not, in other words, have taken an HIV test. Even if he had been able to, there was little that could be done for him. The antibiotics he was prescribed could do little more than relieve some of his symptoms. It was not until 1987 that GlaxoSmithKlein was licensed to market the first effective anti-HIV drug.

Foucault cannot have known a great deal about his condition, but there are minor indications that he did know that something was seriously wrong. When he travelled to Poland in September 1982, he left a letter 'to be opened in case of accident'. He died without leaving a proper will, and the letter was interpreted as being an expression of his last wishes. Its provisions were simple. The apartment and its contents were to go to Daniel Defert, and there were to be 'no posthumous publications'. More enigmatically, it also read 'Death, not invalidity'.

A further scandal broke in 1990 when Hervé Guibert published his novel *A L'Ami qui ne m'a pas sauvé la vie*. Like all Guibert's fiction, it is largely autobiographical but it also paints a disturbing portrait of Foucault that shocked many people. Foucault is thinly disguised as Muzil, and Defert as 'Stéphane'. The name 'Muzil' is a direct allusion to Robert Musil and his *Man Without Qualities*, a novel enjoyed by both Foucault and Guibert. The 'Muzil' figure certainly knows what he is suffering from, and seems to look forward to his own death as though it were some dark apotheosis. That, however, is neither the most disturbing nor the most scandalous feature of Guibert's novel. It is the portrait of a man who 'adored violent orgies in saunas' and who would quietly slip out at night, dressed in leather to look for 'victims' at Le Keller, a well-known gay bar near the place de la République.[29] This is a man who discovered the delights of sado-masochism in California and who kept whips and chains in his apartment. The revelation of a sado-masochistic Foucault is in fact less startling than many readers thought:

Foucault hinted at his inclinations in some of the interviews given in the 1980s, although it is true that they were not all easy to locate at the time. The overall accuracy of the portrait is hard to dispute, though the details are no doubt exaggerated. Guibert spent a lot of time with Foucault in 1983–4 and passages in the novel are clearly based on entries in the journal he kept from 1976 to 1991, when he too died of AIDS.[30]

In the autumn of 1984 Daniel Defert poured his energy and organizational skills into something new by founding AIDES, which was France's first association for people with AIDS. The pun was deliberate: it alludes to the English term for what the French call SIDA, and plays on the verb *aider* ('to help'). It was set up to provide material, financial and above all moral support for victims of HIV and AIDS. Commenting on Aron's remarks about Foucault's supposed shame, Defert remarked: 'If we had, as Aron says, been ashamed, I would never have created AIDES.'[31]

References

One

1 This chapter in particular draws upon interviews carried out while researching my *Lives of Michel Foucault* (London, 1993). Additional information from Denys Foucault and Louis Girard is drawn from interviews published in *L'Actualité Poitou-Charentes*, 51, n. d. The chronology prepared for the first of the four volumes of Michel Foucault's *Dits et écrits* (Paris, 1994) is an essential point of reference. See also Didier Eribon, *Michel Foucault* (Paris, 1989) and James Miller, *The Passion of Michel Foucault* (London, 1993). Unless otherwise stated, all translations from French are my own.

2 'Radioscopie de Michel Foucault' (radio interview with Jacques Chancel, October 1975), in *Dits et écrits*, vol. I, p. 783.

3 'The Minimalist Self' (English-language interview with Stephen Riggins, 1983) in Michel Foucault, *Politics, Philosophy, Culture: Selected Writings, 1977–1984*, ed. Lawrence D. Kritzman (London and New York, 1988), pp. 3–4.

4 Michel Foucault, *L'Herméneutique du sujet: cours au Collège de France, 1981–1982* (Paris, 2001), p. 325.

5 Michel Foucault, 'Veilleur de la nuit des hommes' (1963), in *Dits et écrits*, vol. I, p. 230.

6 'The Minimalist Self', p. 7.

7 Michel Foucault, 'Jean Hyppolite, 1907–1968', *Dits et écrits*, vol. I, p 179.

8 'Qui êtes-vous, professeur Foucault?' (interview with P. Caruso, 1967), in *Dits et écrits*, vol. I, p. 606; unpublished interview (1966), cited in Philippe Artières, 'Dire l'actualité', in *Foucault: le courage de la vérité*, ed. Frédéric Gros (Paris, 2002), p. 24.

9 Friedrich Nietzsche, *Ecce Homo*, trans. R. J. Hollingdale
   (Harmondsworth, 1979), p. 69.

10 Michel Foucault, 'Sur les façons d'écrire l'histoire' (interview with
   Raymond Bellour, 1967), in *Dits et écrits*, vol. I, p. 595.

11 'De l'Amitié comme mode de vie' (interview with R. de Ceccary. J. Danet
   and J. Le Bitoux, 1981), in *Dits et écrits*, vol. IV, pp. 163–4.

12 'The Minimalist Self', pp. 11–12.

Two

1 Michel Foucault, 'Le vrai sexe' (1980), in *Dits et écrits* (Paris, 1994), vol.
   IV, p. 122. This is a version of the text first published as the introduction
   to Richard MacDougal's translation of *Herculine Barbin* (Brighton, 1980).

2 Maurice Pinguet, 'Les Années d'apprentissage', *Le Débat*, 41
   (September–October 1986), pp. 122, 124.

3 See *Economy & Society*, XVII/2–3 (1990). Special issue on 'Society and the
   Life Sciences: In Honour of Georges Canguilhem'.

4 Pinguet, 'Les Années d'apprentissage', p. 127.

5 Cited in Otto Friedrich, 'France's Philosopher of Power', *Time*,
   6 November 1981, pp. 147–8.

6 Emmanuel Leroy Ladurie, *Paris–Montpellier, PCF–PSU, 1945–1963* (Paris,
   1982), pp. 165–6.

7 Michel Foucault, 'La folie n'existe que dans une société' (interview with
   J.-P. Weber, 1961), in *Dits et écrits*, vol. I, p. 167.

8 'Introduction', in Ludwig Binswanger, *Le Rêve et l'existence* (Paris, 1954);
   also in *Dits et écrits*, vol. I, pp. 65–118. Translated as Michel Foucault and
   Ludwig Binswanger, *Dream and Existence*, ed. Keith Holler (Atlantic
   Highlands, NJ, 1993).

9 See in particular his introduction to Carolyn Fawcett's translation of
   Georges Canguilhem, *On the Normal and the Pathological* (Boston, MA,
   1978).

10 Michel Foucault, *Maladie mentale et personnalité* (Paris, 1954). The
   English translation by Alan Sheridan, *Mental Illness and Psychology*
   (New York, 1976), is of the second, revised edition.

11 Jean-Paul Aron, *Les Modernes* (Paris, 1984), pp. 72–4.

12 English translation, *The Death of Virgil* by Jean Starr Untermeyer (New

York, 1945).

13 'Qui êtes-vous, professeur Foucault?' (interview with P. Caruso, 1967), in
Dits et écrits, vol. I, p. 613.

14 Michel Foucault and Pierre Boulez, 'La Musique contemporaine et le
public' (1983), in *Dits et écrits*, vol. IV, pp. 480–95; 'Quelques souvenirs de
Pierre Boulez', ed. Alain Joubert, *Critique*, XLII, 471–772, pp. 745–7.

15 'Postscript', Michel Foucault, *Death and the Labyrinth: The World of
Raymond Roussel*, trans. Charles Ruas (London, 1987), p. 174.

16 Maurice Pinguet, 'Les Années d'apprentissage', p. 130.

17 Friedrich Nietzsche, *The Gay Science*, trans. Walter Kaufmann (New York,
1974), p. 81.

18 http://www.bellefroid.com/chambre_fs.htm

19 Michel Foucault, 'La psychologie de 1850 à 1950', in *Dits et écrits*, vol. I,
pp. 120–37.

Three

1 Georges Dumézil, 'Un homme heureux', *Le Nouvel Observateur*, 29 June
1984, p. 42; *Entretiens avec Didier Eribon* (Paris, 1987), p. 214.

2 'Interview avec Michel Foucault' (interview with C. G. Bjurström, 1968),
in *Dits et écrits* (Paris, 1994), vol. I, p. 651.

3 'The Minimalist Self' (English-language interview with Stephen Riggins,
1983) in Michel Foucault, *Politics, Philosophy, Culture: Selected Writings,
1977–1984*, ed. Lawrence D. Kritzman (London and New York, 1988), p. 5.

4 Michel Foucault, 'Truth, Power, Self' (interview with Rux Martin, 1982),
in *Technologies of the Self: A Seminar with Michel Foucault*, ed. Luther H.
Martin, Huck Gutman and Patrick H. Hutton (London, 1988), p. 9.

5 See Jean-Louis Calvet, *Roland Barthes: A Biography*, trans. Sarah Wykes
(Cambridge, 1994).

6 Jean Barraqué, *Ecrits*, ed. Laurent Fenneyrou (Paris, 2001), p. 26.

7 'Entretien avec Michel Foucault' (interview with Ducio Trombador, late
1978), in *Dits et écrits*, vol. IV, p. 78.

8 Etienne Burin des Roziers, 'Une rencontre à Varsovie', *Le Débat*, 41
(September–October 1986), pp. 132–6.

9 *Dits et écrits*, vol. IV, p. 344

10 Pierre Gascar, 'La Nuit de Sankt Pauli', in *Portraits et souvenirs* (Paris,

1991), pp. 63–94.

11 Cited in Didier Eribon, *Michel Foucault* (Paris, 1989), p. 155.

12 Preface to first edition of *Folie et déraison* (Paris, 1961), in *Dits et écrits*, vol. I, p. 167.

13 Immanuel Kant, *Anthropologie du point de vue pragmatique*, trans. Michel Foucault (Paris, 1988).

14 Michel Foucault and Arlette Farge, 'Le Style de l'histoire', *Libération*, 21 February 1981, p. 20.

15 See Philippe Ariès, *Un historien du dimanche* (Paris, 1980).

16 Michel Foucault, *Folie et déraison: histoire de la folie à l'âge classique* (Paris, 1961); trans. by Richard Howard as *Madness and Civilisation: A History of Insanity in the Age of Reason* (London, 1967). The translation is of the abridged 1964 version.

17 'La Folie n'existe que dans une société', *Dits et écrits*, vol. I, pp. 167–9.

Four

1 Claude Mauriac, *Et comme l'espérance est violente* (Paris, 1986), p. 595.

2 On the literary Foucault, see Simon During, *Foucault and Literature: Towards a Genealogy of Writing* (London, 1992).

3 'Postscript' to Michel Foucault, *Death and the Labyrinth: The World of Raymond Roussel*, trans. Charles Ruas (London, 1987), p. 185.

4 Michel Foucault, *Naissance de la clinique* (Paris, 1963); trans. by A. M. Sheridan as *The Birth of the Clinique* (London, 1973).

5 Jacques Derrida, 'Cogito et histoire de la folie', in *L'Ecriture et la différence* (Paris, 1967), pp. 51–99.

6 On Foucault and *Critique*, see Sylvie Patron, *Critique, 1946–1996: une encyclopédie de l'esprit moderne* (Paris, 1999).

7 Michel Foucault, *Dits et écrits* (Paris, 1994), vol. I, pp. 233–49. On Bataille, see Michael Richardson, *Georges Bataille* (London, 1994).

8 Michel Foucault, *Les Mots et les choses* (Paris, 1966); as *The Order of Things* (London, 1970).

9 *Le Nouvel Observateur*, 10 August 1966, p. 58.

10 Michel Foucault, *L'Archéologie du savoir* (Paris, 1969); trans. by A. M. Sheridan Smith as *The Archaeology of Knowledge* (London, 1972).

11 Michel Foucault, 'C'était un nageur entre deux eaux' (October 1966), in

Dits et écrits, vol. I, pp. 554–7.

12 Marc Beigbeder, 'En suivant le cours de Foucault', *Esprit*, June 1967, pp. 1066–9.

13 'Jean-Paul Sartre répond', *L'Arc*, 40 (October 1966), pp. 87–96; Michel Foucault, 'L'Homme est-il mort?' (interview with Claude Bonnefoy, 1966), in *Dits et écrits*, vol. I, pp. 540–44.

14 Jean Daniel, *La Blessure* (Paris, 1992), pp. 168–9.

15 Pinguet, 'Les Années d'apprentissage', p. 126.

16 Jean Daniel, 'La Passion de Michel Foucault', *Le Nouvel Observateur*, 24 June 1984.

Five

1 Maurice Blanchot, *Foucault tel que je l'imagine* (Montpellier, 1986), p. 9.

2 Michel Foucault, *L'Archéologie du savoir* (Paris, 1969), p. 28.

3 'Entretien avec Michel Foucault', *Dits et écrits* (Paris, 1994), vol. IV, p. 71.

4 'Prisons et asiles dans le mécanisme du pouvoir' (1974), in *Dits et écrits*, vol. II, p. 524.

5 See Hervé Hamon and Patrick Rotman, *Génération. 2, Les Années de Poudre* (Paris, 1988); Christophe Bouseiller, *Les Maoïstes: la folle histoire des gardes rouges français* (Paris, 1996).

6 See Robert Linhart, *L'Etabli* (Paris, 1978); Virginie Linhart, *Volontaires pour l'usine: vies d'établis, 1967–1977* (Paris, 1994).

7 Michel Foucault, 'Le Piège de Vincennes', *Dits et écrits*, vol. II, pp. 67–74.

8 Michel Foucault, 'Mon corps, ce papier, ce feu', *Dits et écrits*, vol. II, pp. 245–67.

9 'Titres et travaux', *Dits et écrits*, vol. I, pp. 842–6.

10 Michel Foucault, *L'Ordre du discours* (Paris, 1971), pp. 7, 81–2.

11 Michel Foucault, *'Il faut défendre la société'* (Paris, 1997), pp. 3–4; trans. by David Macey as *'Society Must Be Defended'* (London, 2003).

12 A full documentary account is given in Le Groupe d'Information sur les Prisons, *Archives d'une lutte* (Paris, 2003).

13 See Serge Livrozet, *De la prison à la révolte* (Paris, 1973).

14 See 'Les Intellectuels et le pouvoir' (interview with G. Deleuze, 1972), in *Dits et écrits*, vol. III, pp. 306–15.

15 Printed as a paid advertisement in *Le Monde*, 26–7 December 1971.

16 See Philippe Artières, '1972: Naissance de l'intellectuel spécifique', *Plein Droit*, 53–4 (March 2002).

17 See in particular his *Et comme l'espérance est violente* (Paris, 1986).

18 See Véronique Vasseur, *Médecin-chef à la Prison de la Santé* (Paris, 2000).

19 See FHAR, *Rapport contre la normalité* (Paris, 1971). For a general account, see Frédéric Martel, *Le Rose et le noir: les homosexuels en France depuis 1968* (Paris, 1996).

20 See Bill Marshall, *Guy Hocquenghem: Theorising the Gay Nation* (London, 1996).

Six

1 See 'Sur la justice populaire: débat avec les maos', *Dits et écrits* (Paris, 1994), vol. IV, pp. 340–68.

2 For a fictionalized account, see Dominique Rolin, *Tigre en papier* (Paris, 2002).

3 Louis Althusser, *L'Avenir dure longtemps* (Paris, 1992), pp. 224–5.

4 Michel Foucault, *Les Anormaux: cours au Collège de France, 1974–1975* (Paris, 1999).

5 See *Moi, Pierre Rivière, ayant égorgé ma mere, ma soeur et mon frère . . . un cas de parricide au XIXe siècle présenté par Michel Foucault* (Paris, 1973).

6 *Les Machines à guérir (Aux Origines de l'hôpital moderne). Dossier présenté par Michel Foucault, Blandine Barret Kriegel, Anne Thalamy, François Beguin,Brunto Fortier* (Brussels and Liège, 1977); Georges Canguilhem, 'Les Machines à guérir', *Le Monde*, 6 April 1977.

7 See Michel Foucault, *'Il faut défendre la société'* (Paris, 1997).

8 Michel Foucault, *L'Herméneutique du sujet: cours au Collège de France, 1981–1982* (Paris, 2001), p. 378.

9 Cited in Claude Mauriac, *Mauriac et fils* (Paris, 1986), p. 222; 'Qui êtes-vous, professeur Foucault?' (interview with P. Caruso, 1967), in *Dits et écrits*, vol. I, p. 607.

10 Cited in Claude Mauriac, *Et comme l'espérance est violente* (Paris, 1986), pp. 59–91.

11 'Asiles, sexualité, prisons', *Dits et écrits*, vol. II, p. 775.

12 'Vat-t-on extrader Klaus Croissant', *Dits et écrits*, vol. III, pp. 361–5.

13 Jean Genet, 'Violence et brutalité', *Le Monde*, 2 September 1977.

14 Cited in Mauriac, *Et comme l'espérance est violente*, pp. 590–91.

15 Michel Foucault, *Surveiller et punir* (Paris, 1975); trans. by Alan Sheridan as *Discipline and Punish* (London, 1977). See Ernst H. Kantorowicz, *The King's Two Bodies: A Study in Medieval Political Theology* (Princeton, NJ, 1957).

16 Jeremy Bentham, *Le Panoptique* (Paris, 1977).

17 Gilles Deleuze and Félix Guattari, *Anti-Oedipe* (Paris, 1972).

18 Steven Marcus, *The Other Victorians: A Study of Pornography and Sexuality in Mid-Nineteenth-Century England* (London, 1966).

19 Michel Foucault, *La Volonté de savoir* (Paris, 1976); trans. by Robert Hurley as *The History of Sexuality. Volume I: An Introduction* (London, 1979).

20 Michel Foucault, 'Non au sexe roi', *Dits et écrits*, vol. III, pp. 261–2.

21 Foucault, 'Non au sexe roi', vol. III, pp. 261–2. On Guibert, see François Buot, *Hervé Guibert, le jeune homme et la mort* (Paris, 1999); Christian Solell, *Hervé Guibert* (Saint-Etienne, 2002).

22 'La Grande Colère des faits', *Dits et écrits*, vol. III, pp. 277–81.

23 'Un plaisir simple', *Dits et écrits*, vol. III, pp. 777–9.

Seven

1 See 'Le Gai Savoir II', *Mec Magazine*, 6–7 (July–August 1988), pp. 30–33. This text is not included in Michel Foucault, *Dits et écrits* (Paris, 1994).

2 Michel Foucault and Richard Sennett, 'Sexuality and solitude', *London Review of Books*, 21 May–3 June 1981, p. 5.

3 *Corriere della Sera*, 28 September 1978.

4 'A Quoi rêvent les Iraniens?', *Dits et écrits*, vol. II, pp. 688–95.

5 See in particular 'Le Chef mythique de la révolte de l'Iran' and 'Téhéran: la foi contre le chah', in *Dits et écrits*, vol. III, pp. 713–16, pp. 683–7.

6 'Lettre ouverte à Mehdi Bazargan', *Dits et écrits*, pp. 780–83.

7 For a full account, see Bernard Kouchner, *L'Ile de lumière* (Paris, 1989).

8 Claude Mauriac, *Mauriac et fils* (Paris, 1986), p. 226.

9 'Roland Barthes (12 novembre 1915–26 mars 1980)', *Dits et écrits*, vol. IV, p. 125.

10 'The Minimalist Self' (English-language interview with Stephen Riggins, 1983) in Michel Foucault, *Politics, Philosophy, Culture: Selected Writings*,

1977–1984, ed. Lawrence D. Kritzman (London and New York, 1988), p. 12.

11 Katarina von Bülow, 'Contredire est un devoir', *Le Débat*, 41 (September–October 1986), p. 177.

12 Pierre Nora, 'Que peuvent les intellectuels?', *Le Débat*, 1 May 1980, pp. 3–19.

13 Roger Knobelspiess, QHS: *Quartier de Haute Sécurité* (Préface de Michel Foucault), (Paris, 1980).

14 Sterling McMurrin, ed., *The Tanner Lecture on Human Values* (Salt Lake City, 1981). Unpublished transcripts of the Howinson Lectures can be consulted at IMEC, Paris.

15 See 'Michel Foucault, An Interview: Sex, Power and the Politics of Identity', *The Advocate*, 400 (7 August 1984).

16 Friedrich Nietzsche, *The Gay Science*, trans. Walter Kaufmann (New York, 1974), p. 232.

17 Michel Foucault, *L'Usage des plaisirs* (Paris, 1984), p. 63; trans. by Robert Hurley as *The Use of Pleasure* (London, 1986).

18 Michel Foucault, *Le souci de soi* (Paris, 1984); trans. by Robert Hurley as *The Care of the Self* (London, 1988).

19 *Le Désordre des familles. Lettres de cachet des Archives de la Bastille. Présenté par Arlette Farge et Michel Foucault* (Paris, 1982).

20 Guy Hocquenghem, *Lettre ouverte à ceux qui sont passés du col Mao au Rotary* (Paris, 1986).

21 Max Gallo, 'Les Intellectuels, la politique et la modernité', *Le Monde*, 26 July 1983.

22 Pierre Bourdieu and Michel Foucault, 'Les Rendez-vous manqués', *Libération*, 15 December 1981.

23 Cited in Bernard Kouchner, 'Un vrai samurai', *Michel Foucault: une histoire de la vérité* (Paris, 1985), p. 88.

24 'Foucault: Non aux compromis', *Dits et écrits*, vol. IV, pp. 336–7.

25 Cited in Philip Horvits, 'Don't cry for me, Academia', *Jimmy and Lucy's House of K 2*, August 1984, p. 80; cited in Gregory Woods, 'La Fin d'Arcadie: *Gai Pied* and the "Cancer gai"', *French Cultural Studies*, IX (1998), p. 299.

26 Alan Sheridan, 'Diary', *London Review of Books*, 19 July–1 August 1984, p. 21.

27 Hocquenghem, *Lettre ouverte*, p. 119.

28 Jean-Paul Aron, 'Mon SIDA', *Le Nouvel Observateur*, 30 October 1987.

29 Guibert, *A L'Ami qui ne m'a as sauvé la vie*, [[AQ: place/date ?]] pp. 117–18.

30 Hervé Guibert, *Le Mausolée des amants: Journal 1976–1991* (Paris, 2001).

31 'Daniel Defert: plus on est honteux, plus on avoue', *Libération*, 31 October–1 November 1987, p. 2.

Select Bibliography

Works by Michel Foucault

Maladie mentale et personnalité (Paris, 1954)

'Introduction' to Ludwig Binswanger, *Le Rêve et l'existence*, trans. Jacqueline Verdeaux (Paris, 1954)

Folie et déraison: histoire de la folie à l'âge classique (Paris, 1961)

Maladie mentale et psychologie (Paris, 1966)

Naissance de la clinique: une archéologie de regard médical (Paris, 1963)

Raymond Roussel (Paris, 1963)

Les Mots et les choses: une archéologie des sciences humaines (Paris, 1966)

L'Archéologie du savoir (Paris, 1969)

L'Ordre du discours (Paris, 1970)

'Présentation', *Moi, Pierre Rivière, ayant égorgé ma mère, ma sœur et mon frère . . . un cas de parricide au XIXe siècle présenté par Michel Foucault* (Paris, 1973)

Surveiller et punir (Paris, 1975)

Histoire de la sexualité, 1: la volonté de savoir (Paris, 1976)

'Note', *Herculine Barbin dite Alexandre B, présenté par Michel Foucault* (Paris, 1978)

Le Désordre des familles: lettres de cachet des Archives de la Bastille. Présenté par Arlette Farge et Michel Foucault (Paris, 1982)

Histoire de la sexualité, 2: l'usage de plaisirs (Paris, 1984)

Histoire de la sexualité, 3: le souci de soi (Paris, 1984)

'Il Faut défendre la société': cours au Collège de France, 1976 (Paris, 1997)

Les Anormaux: cours au Collège de France, 1974–1975 (Paris, 1999)

L'Herméneutique du sujet: cours au Collège de France, 1981–1982 (Paris, 2001)

Le Pouvoir psychiatrique: cours au Collège de France, 1972–1973 (Paris, 2003)

No collection of Foucault's occasional writings appeared in French during his lifetime. All his published uncollected texts, with the exception of some material published without his authorization, are now available in the four volumes of *Dits et écrits: edition établie sous la direction de Daniel Defert et François Ewald* (Paris, 1994).

Works by Michel Foucault in English translation

Madness and Civilization: A History of Insanity in the Age of Reason, trans. Richard Howard (London, 1967)

Mental Illness and Psychology, trans. Alan Sheridan (Berkeley, CA, 1987)

The Birth of the Clinic: An Archaeology of Medical Perception, trans. Alan Sheridan-Smith (London, 1973)

Death and the Labyrinth: The World of Raymond Roussel, trans. Charles Ruas (London, 1987)

The Order of Things (London, 1971)

The Archaeology of Knowledge, trans. A. M. Sheridan Smith (London, 1972)

I, Pierre Rivière, Having Slaughtered My Mother, My Sister and My Brother. . . , trans. Frank Jellinek (New York, 1975)

Discipline and Punish, trans. Alan Sheridan (London, 1977)

The History of Sexuality, 1: An Introduction, trans. Robert Hurley (New York, 1978)

Herculine Barbin; Being the Recently Discovered Memoirs of a Nineteenth-Century French Hermaphrodite, trans. Richard McDougall (Brighton, 1980)

The Use of Pleasure: The History of Sexuality, Volume 2, trans. Robert Hurley (London, 1988)

The Care of the Self: The History of Sexuality, Volume 3, trans. Robert Hurley (London, 1988)

'Society Must Be Defended': Lectures at the Collège de France, 1975–76, trans. David Macey (London, 2003)

Abnormal: Lectures at the Collège de France, 1974–75, trans. Graham Burchell (London, 2003)

Michel Foucault and Ludwig Binswanger, *Dream and Existence*, ed. Keith Hoeller (Atlantic Heights, NJ, 1993)

Several collections of shorter works and interviews have been published in English translation. With one exception, they have now been superseded by a three-volume collection of *Essential Works*.

Lawrence D. Kritzman, ed., *Michel Foucault: Politics, Philosophy, Culture: Interviews and Other Writings, 1977–1984* (London and New York, 1988)
Paul Rabinow, ed., *Ethics: Subjectivity and Truth. The Essential Works of Michel Foucault, 1985–1984, Volume 1* (London, 1997)
James D. Faubion, ed., *Aesthetics, Method and Epistemology: Essential Works of Foucault, 1984–1984, Volume 2* (London, 1998)
—, *Power: Essential Works of Foucault, 1954–1984, Volume 3* (London, 2001)

On Michel Foucault

The literature on Michel Foucault is now so extensive as to border on the unmanageable. It is also becoming increasingly specialized. All the titles listed here contain at least some introductory material.

James W. Bernauer, *Michel Foucault's Force of Flight: Towards an Ethics for Thought* (Atlantic Heights, NJ, and London, 1990)
Jeremy R. Carrette, *Foucault and Religion: Spiritual Corporality and Political Spirituality* (London and New York, 2000)
Irene Diamond and Lee Quinby, eds, *Foucault and Feminism: Reflections on Resistance* (Boston, MA, 1988)
Hubert L. Dreyfus and Paul Rabinow, *Michel Foucault: Beyond Structuralism and Hermeneutics* (Hemel Hempstead, 1982)
Simon During, *Foucault and Literature: Towards a Genealogy of Writing* (London and New York, 1992)
Didier Eribon, *Michel Foucault*, trans. Betsy Wing (Cambridge, MA, 1991)
Gary Gutting, *Michel Foucault's Archaeology of Scientific Reason* (Cambridge, 1989)
David M. Halperin, *Saint Foucault: Towards a Gay Hagiography* (New York, 1995)
David Couzens Hoy, ed., *Foucault: A Critical Reader* (Oxford, 1986)
Colin Jones and Roy Porter, eds, *Reassessing Foucault: Power, Medicine and the Body* (London and New York, 1994)
Macey, David, *The Lives of Michel Foucault* (London, 1993)

Ricardo Miguel-Alfonso and Silvia Caporale-Bizzini, *Reconstructing Foucault: Essays in the Wake of the '80s* (Amsterdam and Atlanta, GA, 1994)
Sarah Mills, *Michel Foucault* (London, 2003)
John Rajchman, *Michel Foucault: The Freedom of Philosophy* (New York, 1985)
Alan Sheridan, *Michel Foucault: The Will to Truth* (London, 1980)

Internet
The following sites are good source of information, bibliographies and links to other sites.

http://www.theory.org.uk/foucault
http://www.thefoucauldian.co.uk
http://foucault-info
http://www.foucault.qut.edu.au

Photo Acknowledgements

The author and publishers wish to express their thanks to the below sources of illustrative material and/or permission to reproduce it:

Photos courtesy of the author: p. 115; photo J. Bauer/© Jerry Bauer/Opale: p. 119; photo Daniel Defert: 50; photos Fonds Centre Michel Foucault/ Archives IMEC: 50, 77, 96; photo ©FOTOLIB: p. 100; photo Photo12.com/ Carlos Freire: p. 123; photos Sipa Press/Rex Features: pp. 6, 80, 101, 136, 142.